Photoshop 7
IMAGE EFFECTS

Dong Mi Kim, Kwang Woo Baek and Kyung In Jang

Photoshop 7 Image Effects

Korean language edition originally published in Korea in 2002 by Youngjin.com, Seoul, Korea. All rights reserved.

This edition published 2002 by Muska & Lipman, a division of Course Technology.

Credits: Senior Editor, Mark Garvey; Technical Editor, Lisa Bucki; Cover Design, Chad Planner; Interior Design and Layout, Chad Planner; Proofreading, Karen Annett.

Publisher: Andy Shafran.

Library of Congress Catalog Number: 2002115217

ISBN 1-932094-21-0

5 4 3 2 1

Educational facilities, companies, and organizations interested in multiple copies or licensing of this book should contact the publisher for quantity discount information. Training manuals, CD-ROMs, and portions of this book are also available individually or can be tailored for specific needs.

Muska & Lipman Publishing
2645 Erie Avenue, Suite 41
Cincinnati, Ohio 45208
www.muskalipman.com
publisher@muskalipman.com

Photoshop 7 Image Effects

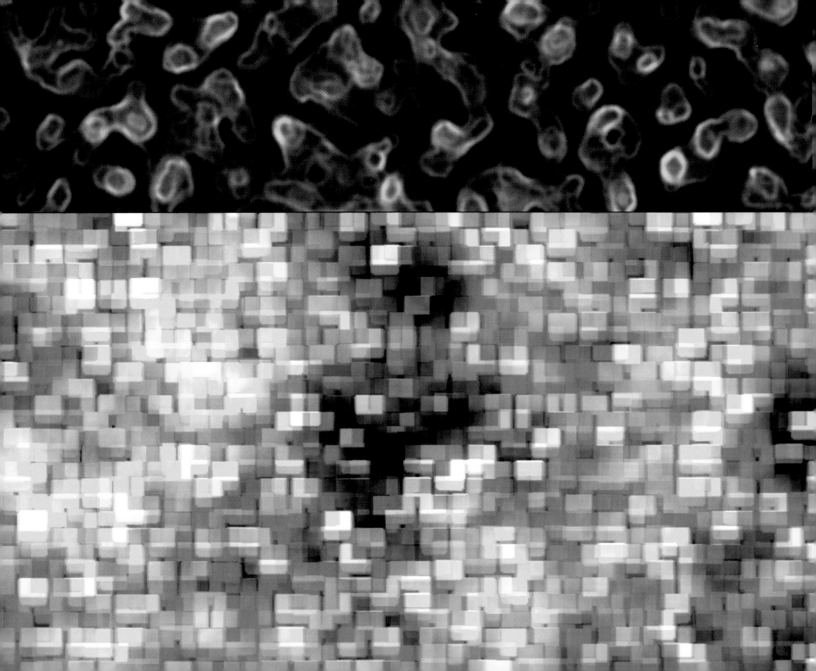

CD-ROM Organization

The CD-ROM

The supplementary CD-ROM contains all of the source elements used to create the images found in this book.

Source Data

All example sources and image files needed are contained on the CD-ROM. You will find them in the "sources" subdirectory.

Projects

Finished projects can be found on the CD-ROM in the "projects" directory.

Contents

Project 1
A Cover Model   2

Project 2
High Contrast   10

Project 3
Woodcut Style
Photograph   20

Project 4
Smile Face   28

Project 5
Basic Photo Repair   38

Project 6
Cross Filter Effect   50

Project 7
Engraving Collage   62

Project 8
Nice Close-Up   74

Project 11
Spring Rain   136

Project 14
Forest Light   162

Project 9
Creative Artwork   86

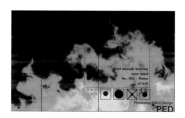

Project 12
Realistic Flame   144

Project 15
A Cube Mosaic   172

Project 10
Photo Collage   108

Project 13
Wire Frame Bridge   152

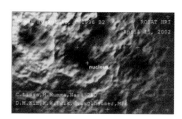

Project 16
Satellite Photography   184

Contents

Project 17
Charcoal Drawing   194

Project 18
Spring Breeze   204

Project 19
Cubic Pipe   216

Project 20
3-D Metallic Spheres
230

Project 21
Type Space   244

Project 22
Blue Distortion   258

Project 23
Bacteria Liquid   272

Project 24
Hard Light Effect   286

Project 25
Backlighted Shot   302

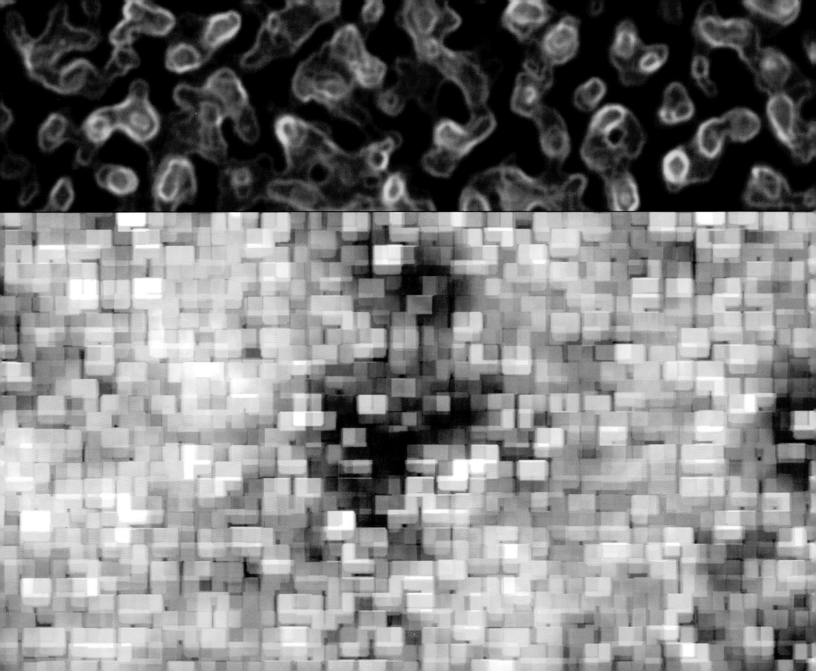

Photoshop 7 Image Effects

With the rapid development of inexpensive digital cameras, everyone from the average person to the professional photographer can capture digital images. Using Photoshop 7.0, you will learn in this book how to correct flaws in digital photographs and how to blend and transform digital photographs to create truly unique results. You will also use Photoshop 7.0's diverse filters and editing features to create unique and creative textures.

auditorium 178

Sun, May 12, 2002
In The Spotlight

The Quartet
has always enjoyed an excellent
with praise concentrating on the
tonal sensitivity and sheer style.

"...Poulenc's Suite Française, the
range of expression from bold, br
to the quietest pianissimo which
to the audience." (Classical Guitar)

Win a Contest · How to kick

Project 1: A Cover Model

In this project, learn how to remove the dark, bluish tint in most photographs to create a picture worthy of a magazine cover. Use layer blending to produce a gorgeous image with vivid color.

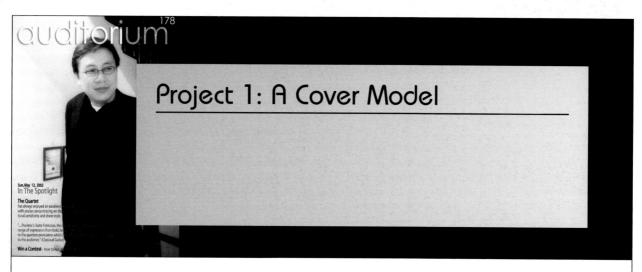

Total Steps

STEP 1. Correcting the Source Photo's Color

STEP 2. Removing Noise from the Image

STEP 3. Copying and Blurring the Layer

STEP 4. Blending the Copied Layer

STEP 5. Copying and Blending another Layer

STEP 6. Adding Text to Complete the Image

STEP 1. Correcting the Source Photo's Color

Choose File, Open (Ctrl/Command+O) and open the Book\Sources\master.jpg file from the supplementary CD-ROM. Copy the Background layer by dragging it onto the Create a new layer button on the Layers palette. Leave the Background copy layer selected in the Layers palette so that your changes will be applied to the layer copy. The fluorescent lighting from the area where the picture was taken gives the image a bluish tint. To correct the color, choose Image, Adjustments, Variations from the menu bar to open the Variations dialog box. Click the More Yellow and More Red image thumbnails until you achieve the desired color, and then click OK to apply the changes to the copied layer.

master.jpg

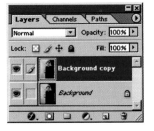

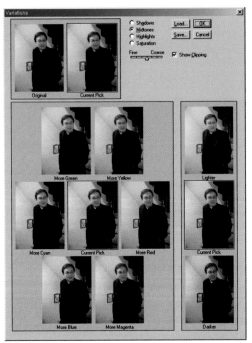

STEP 2.
Removing Noise from the Image

Choose Filter, Noise, Median from the menu bar to open the Median dialog box. Set the Radius to 1, and then click OK to remove unnecessary noise and particles from the image.

STEP 3. Copying and Blurring the Layer

Copy the original Background layer by dragging it onto the Create a new layer button on the Layers palette. Drag the new layer, Background copy 2, above the Background copy layer in the Layers palette. With the Background copy 2 layer still selected, choose Filter, Blur, Gaussian Blur from the menu bar to open the Gaussian Blur dialog box. Set the Radius to 1, and then click OK to blur the image.

STEP 4. Blending the Copied Layer

With the Background copy 2 layer still selected in the Layers palette, click the Add a layer style button, and then click Blending Options. Choose Screen from the Blend Mode drop-down list in the Layer Style dialog box, and then click OK to brighten the areas where the colors of the two layers mix.

STEP 5.
Copying and Blending another Layer

Copy the original Background layer again by dragging it onto the Create a new layer button on the Layers palette. Drag the new Background copy 3 layer to the top of the Layers palette, above the Background copy 2 layer. With the Background copy 3 layer still selected in the Layers palette, click the Add a layer style button, and then click Blending Options. Choose Soft Light from the Blend Mode drop-down list in the Layer Style dialog box, and then click OK to soften the image.

STEP 6. Adding Text to Complete the Image

Choose the Horizontal Type tool from the toolbox, and then click the Toggle the Character and Paragraph palettes button on the Options bar to open the Character palette. Adjust the palette settings as shown here, click on the image and type the word "auditorium" across the top, and then click the Commit any current edits button on the Options bar. With the new auditorium text layer still selected in the Layers palette, click the Add a layer style button, and then click Drop Shadow. Adjust the settings in the Layer Style dialog box as desired, and then click OK. Use the Fill slider on the Layers palette to change the Fill value for the auditorium layer to 64%. Complete the image by using the Horizontal Type tool and the Character palette to add the text shown in the bottom-left corner of the image.

Project 2: High Contrast

In this project, take a very natural picture and give it a mysterious feel by enhancing the image contrast. Also learn the techniques for removing and enhancing selected areas of the image.

High Contrast

Project 2: High Contrast

Total Steps

STEP 1.   Correcting the Source Photo's Color

STEP 2.   Copying and Blurring the Layer

STEP 3.   Blending the Copied Layer

STEP 4.   Copying the Layer to Emphasize the Contrast

STEP 5.   Restoring the Area Around the Mouth

STEP 6.   Removing Unnecessary Areas of the Image

STEP 7.   Adding Orange Vertical Strips

STEP 8.   Adding Text to Complete the Image

ice_cone.jpg

STEP 1. Correcting the Source Photo's Color

Choose File, Open (Ctrl/Command+O) and open the Book\Sources\ice_cone.jpg file from the supplementary CD-ROM. The picture is slightly dark with strong bluish overtones because the picture was taken late in the day. Correct the color of the Background layer by choosing Image, Adjustments, Auto Color from the menu bar.

STEP 2. Copying and Blurring the Layer

Copy the Background layer by dragging it onto the Create a new layer button on the Layers palette. Leave the new Background copy layer selected in the Layers palette. Choose Filter, Blur, Gaussian Blur from the menu bar to open the Gaussian Blur dialog box. Set the Radius to 4, and then click OK to blur the copied layer.

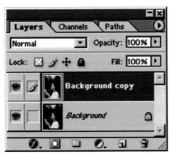 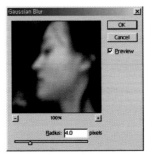 

STEP 3. Blending the Copied Layer

With the Background copy layer still selected in the Layers palette, click the Add a layer style button, and then click Blending Options. Choose Overlay from the Blend Mode drop-down list in the Layer Style dialog box, and then click OK to create strong contrast and raise the hue.

STEP 4. Copying the Layer to Emphasize the Contrast

Make two copies of the Background copy layer by dragging that layer onto the Create a new layer button in the Layers palette. This emphasizes the contrast so that the background is almost black and the foreground is almost all white. Strong contrast appears where the outline of the woman meets the background, with the blurring from the filter making the light appear to spread. Because this effect emphasizes the woman's contours and features, the image takes on a mysterious touch.

STEP 5. Restoring the Area Around the Mouth

You can see that the lips and the chin blend too much into the background. Choose the Dodge tool from the toolbox. Working on the Background copy 3 layer, drag from the front of the woman's lips out into the background. The Dodge tool will lighten this area so that the lips become more prominent and the face appears more natural. If the effect is still too weak, use the Dodge tool on the same area in the Background copy 2 layer. Click the palette menu button in the upper-right corner of the Layers palette, and choose Flatten Image to merge all the layers into the Background layer.

STEP 6. Removing Unnecessary Areas of the Image

Choose the Rectangular Marquee tool from the toolbox, and then select the portion of the image shown in the first illustration for this step. Choose Image, Crop to remove the content outside the selection from the image file. Choose Select, Deselect (Ctrl/Command+D) to remove the selection marquee. Click the Default Foreground and Background Colors button on the toolbox to reset the foreground color to black. Choose the Paint Brush tool from the toolbox, and then click the Click to open the Brush Preset picker button on the Options bar. Double-click on the desired brush size in the palette that appears. Then use the brush to color the hand and ice cream cone black, so they disappear from the image. Also use the brush to darken any light areas around the woman's head as desired.

STEP 7. Adding Orange Vertical Strips

Click the Create a new layer button (Shift+Ctrl/Command+N) on the Layers palette to add a new layer named Layer 1. Choose the Rectangular Marquee tool from the toolbox, and select the three areas shown here in yellow. (After you select the first area, press and hold the Shift key as you make the other two selections.) Using the Color palette, set the foreground color to gold (R:255, G:190, B:0) as shown here. Use the Paint Bucket tool or press Alt/Option+Del to fill the selection marquee with the gold foreground color. Choose Select, Deselect to remove the selection marquee.

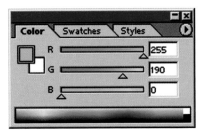

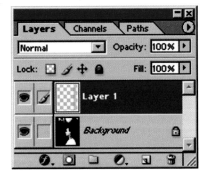

STEP 8. Adding Text to Complete the Image

Choose the Horizontal Type tool from the toolbox, and then click the Toggle the Character and Paragraph palettes button on the Options bar to open the Character palette. Adjust the palette settings as shown here, click on the image and type the word "MONOLOGUE," and then click the Commit any current edits button on the Options bar. With the new MONOLOGUE layer selected in the Layers palette, choose Edit, Free Transform (Ctrl/Command+T) from the menu bar and use the handles that appear to rotate, size, and position the text as shown here. Press Enter/Return to finish the transformation. Complete the image by using the Horizontal Type tool and the Character palette to add the text shown in the finished image here.

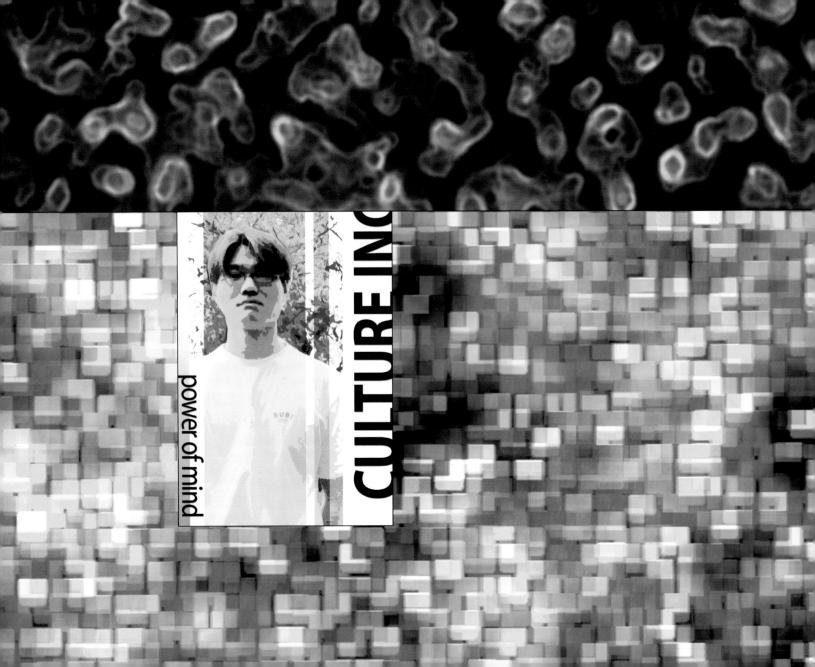

Project 3: Woodcut Style Photograph

Learn how to make a dark photograph appear as if it has been carved on wood. In this project, complete a series of simple steps to achieve the woodcut effect for a truly spectacular poster. By making the color of the person in the image different from the color of the background image, you can emphasize the person in the photograph.

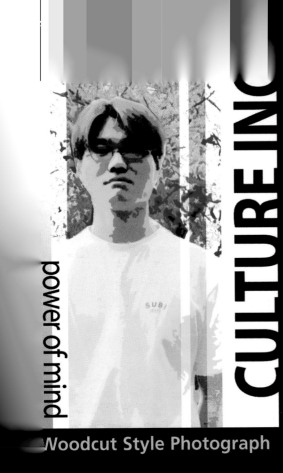

power of mind

CULTURE INC

Woodcut Style Photograph

power of mind

CULTURE INC

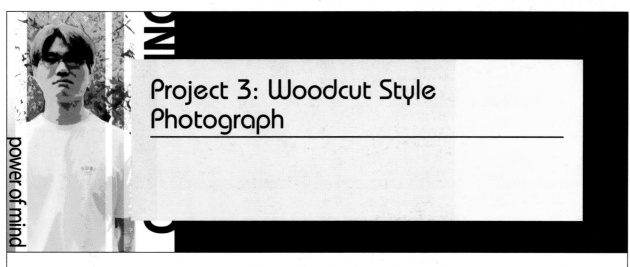

Project 3: Woodcut Style Photograph

Total Steps

STEP 1.   Correcting the Source Photo's Brightness

STEP 2.   Adding Cutout Effects to the Image

STEP 3.   Strengthening the Image Color

STEP 4.   Copying the Man to a New Layer

STEP 5.   Changing the Man's Color

STEP 6.   Blending the Original Image

STEP 7.   Adding and Blending White Vertical Strips

STEP 8.   Adding a Solid White Strip

STEP 9.   Adding Text to Complete the Image

STEP 10. The Final Step

STEP 1. Correcting the Source Photo's Brightness

Choose File, Open (Ctrl/Command+O) and open the Book\Sources\man_pose.jpg file from the supplementary CD-ROM. Choose Image, Adjustments, Levels (Ctrl/Command+L) from the menu bar to open the Levels dialog

man_pose.jpg

 box. Drag the middle Input Levels slider to the left as shown here, and then click OK to brighten the image.

STEP 2. Adding Cutout Effects to the Image

Copy the Background layer by dragging it onto the Create a new layer button on the Layers palette. With the new Background copy layer selected in the Layers palette, choose Filter, Artistic, Cutout from the menu bar to open the Cutout dialog box. Adjust the dialog box settings as shown here, and then click OK to simplify the image.

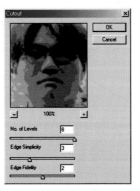

STEP 3.
Strengthening the Image Color

With the Background copy layer still selected, choose Image, Adjustments, Hue/Saturation (Ctrl/Command+U). Drag the sliders in the Hue/Saturation dialog box to the settings shown here, and then click OK.

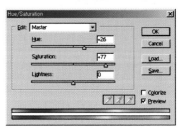

STEP 4. Copying the Man to a New Layer

Choose the Polygonal Lasso tool from the toolbox, and then select the man in the image as shown here. Press Ctrl/Command+C to copy the selection, and then press Ctrl/Command+V to copy the selection into a new layer named Layer 1.

STEP 5. Changing the Man's Color

With the Layer 1 layer still selected in the Layers palette, choose Image, Adjustments, Hue/Saturation (Ctrl/Command+U) from the menu bar. Drag the sliders in the Hue/Saturation dialog box to the settings shown here, and then click OK. This gives the man an orange hue.

STEP 6.
Blending the Original Image

Copy the Background layer by dragging it onto the Create a new layer button on the Layers palette. Drag the new Background copy 2 layer to the top of the Layers palette. With the Background copy 2 layer still selected in the Layers palette, click the Add a layer style button, and then click Blending Options. Choose Overlay from the Blend Mode drop-down list in the Layer Style dialog box, and then click OK to mix layer colors evenly.

STEP 7. Adding and Blending White Vertical Strips

Click the Create a new layer button (Shift+Ctrl/Command+N) on the Layers palette to add a new layer named Layer 2. Choose the Rectangular Marquee tool from the toolbox, and select the three areas shown here in white. (After you select the first area, press and hold the Shift key as you make the other two selections.) Using the Color palette, set the foreground color to white (R:255, G:255, B:255). Use the Paint Bucket tool or press Alt/Option+Del to fill the selection marquee with the white foreground color. Choose Select, Deselect to remove the selection marquee. With the Layer 2 layer still selected in the Layers palette, click the Add a layer style button, and then click Blending Options. Choose Overlay from the Blend Mode drop-down list in the Layer Style dialog box, and then click OK to mix layer colors evenly.

STEP 8. Adding a Solid White Strip

Click the Create a new layer button (Shift+Ctrl/Command+N) on the Layers palette to make a new layer named Layer 3. Choose the Rectangular Marquee tool from the toolbox, and select the two areas shown here in white. (After you select the first area, press and hold the Shift key as you make the other selection.) With white still specified as the foreground color, use the Paint Bucket tool or press Alt/Option+Del to fill the selection marquee with white. Choose Select, Deselect to remove the selection marquee.

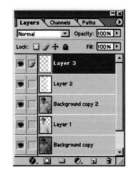

STEP 9. Adding Text to Complete the Image

Click the Default Foreground and Background Colors button in the toolbox to make the foreground color black and the background color white. Choose the Horizontal Type tool from the toolbox, and then click the Toggle the Character and Paragraph palettes button on the Options bar to open the Character palette. Adjust the palette settings as shown here, click on the image and type "CULTURE INC," and then click the Commit any current edits button on the Options bar. With the new CULTURE INC layer selected in the Layers palette, choose Edit, Free Transform (Ctrl/Command+T) from the menu bar and use the handles that appear to rotate, size, and position the text as shown here. Press Enter/Return to finish the transformation. Use the Horizontal Type tool and the Edit, Free Transform command to add and position the "power of mind" text at the left.

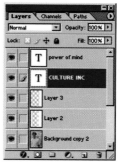

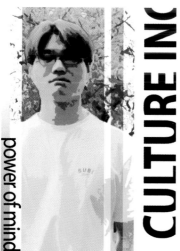

STEP 10. The Final Step

Click the CULTURE INC layer in the Layers palette and then click the Create a new layer button (Shift+Ctrl/Command+N) to make a new layer named Layer 4. Ctrl/Command-click the Layer 3 layer to make a selection on Layer 4 in the shape of the strips on Layer 3. Choose the Rectangular Marquee tool from the toolbox, and press and hold the Alt/Option key while dragging over the right rectangle of the selection marquee to eliminate the right strip from the selection. Choose the Gradient tool from the toolbox, and then drag from the bottom of the selection to the center to apply the gradient. Choose Select, Deselect (Ctrl/Command+D) to remove the selection marquee. With Layer 4 still selected in the Layers palette, use the Fill slider to change the Fill setting for Layer 4 to 26%.

Project 4: Smile Face

Take a picture snapped on the streets using a digital camera
and turn it into an elegant Web image. Using various filters,
such as Cutout and Dry Brush, and various layer blending
modes, you can create a simple yet effective result. A lined
pattern applied to the entire picture makes the image
more elegant.

Take it easy...
Smile
Face

Smile Face

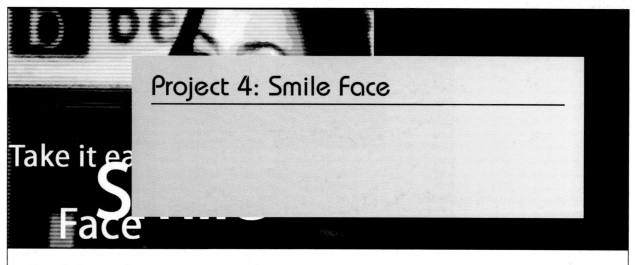

Project 4: Smile Face

Total Steps

STEP 1. Blurring the Source Photo

STEP 2. Applying Cutout Effects to the Image

STEP 3. Applying Brush Effects to the Image

STEP 4. Blending the Layers

STEP 5. Creating the Line Pattern

STEP 6. Filling Layer 1 with the Pattern

STEP 7. Blending the Pattern Layer

STEP 8. Adding a Gradient and Blending the Pattern

STEP 9. Cropping the Image

STEP 10. Adding Text to Complete the Image

STEP 1. Blurring the Source Photo

Choose File, Open (Ctrl/Command+O) and open the Book\Sources\snap.jpg file from the supplementary CD-ROM. Choose Filter, Blur, Gaussian Blur from the menu bar to open the Gaussian Blur dialog box. Set the Radius to approximately 1.4, and then click OK to blur the image slightly and remove fine particles from the picture.

snap.jpg

STEP 2. Applying Cutout Effects to the Image

Copy the Background layer by dragging it onto the Create a new layer button on the Layers palette. Click the eye icon beside the copied layer to hide it from view. Then, click the original Background layer to select it. Choose Filter, Artistic, Cutout to open the Cutout dialog box. Choose the settings shown here, and then click OK. This simplifies the image so it uses fewer colors, as if it were created from colored paper.

 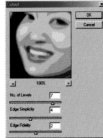 

STEP 3. Applying Brush Effects to the Image

Click the Background copy layer in the Layers palette to both redisplay and select the layer. Choose Filter, Artistic, Dry Brush from the menu bar to open the Dry Brush dialog box. Choose the settings shown here, and then click OK to make the image appear as if it has been painted with a brush.

STEP 4. Blending the Layers

With the Background copy layer still selected in the Layers palette, click the Add a layer style button, and then click Blending Options. Choose Overlay from the Blend Mode drop-down list in the Layer Style dialog box, and then click OK to blend the filter effects applied to the two layers.

STEP 5. Creating the Line Pattern

Click the Create a new layer button (Shift+Ctrl/Command+N) on the Layers palette to add a new layer named Layer 1. Use the Navigator palette to zoom the image to its maximum size (1600%). Click the Default Foreground and Background Colors button on the toolbox to set the foreground color to black. Choose the Pencil tool from the toolbox, and then click the Click to open the Brush Preset picker button on the Options bar. Double-click on the Hard Round 1 pixel brush size to select that brush and close the palette. Drag down to color three pixels black, click the Switch Foreground and Background Colors button on the toolbox to set the foreground color to white, and then drag to color the next three pixels white. This creates a black and white vertical line, as shown here. Ctrl/Command-click on Layer 1 in the Layers palette to make a selection in the shape of the vertical line. Choose Edit, Define Pattern to open the Pattern Name dialog box. Type Stroke as the pattern name, and then click OK to save the selection as a pattern. Choose Select, Deselect (Ctrl/Command+D) to remove the selection marquee.

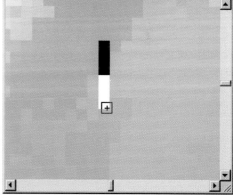

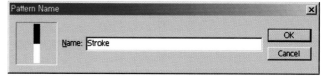

STEP 6. Filling Layer 1 with the Pattern

Choose Edit, Fill from the menu bar to open the Fill dialog box. Choose Pattern from the Use drop-down list, and then click the Custom Pattern box. Double-click the new Stroke pattern to select it and close the palette, and then click OK to fill Layer 1 with the pattern. Use the Navigator palette to zoom back out to 66.67%. The layer has been filled with 3-pixel black and white lines.

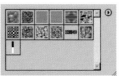
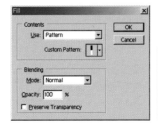

STEP 7. Blending the Pattern Layer

With Layer 1 still selected in the Layers palette, click the Add a layer style button, and then click Blending Options. Choose Color Burn from the Blend Mode drop-down list in the Layer Style dialog box, and then click OK to blend the image of the woman and the striped pattern together naturally. However, the stripes are too dark. Click the Add layer mask button on the Layers palette to add a mask to the layer.

STEP 8. Adding a Gradient and Blending the Pattern

Click the mask thumbnail for Layer 1 in the Layers palette so that an icon identical to the Add layer mask button appears beside the layer. This indicates that you can edit the layer mask. Set the foreground color to white and the background color to black. Choose the Gradient tool from the toolbox, and click the Linear Gradient button on the Options bar, if needed. Then drag from an area above and to the left of the

woman's head down to the just below her chin, as shown here. Applying the gradient to the mask partially hides the pattern. The white areas of the mask image allow the pattern to appear at full intensity, while the darker regions of the mask prevent the pattern from appearing. Then, use the Fill slider on the Layers palette to change the Fill setting for Layer 1 to 70%, further blending the pattern.

STEP 9. Cropping the Image

Choose the Rectangular Marquee tool from the toolbox. Select the portion of the image shown here, and then choose Image, Crop from the menu bar to remove the content outside the selection from the image file. Choose Select, Deselect (Ctrl/Command+D) to remove the selection marquee.

STEP 10. Adding Text to Complete the Image

Complete the image by using the Horizontal Type tool to add the text shown here. Choose a simple font, white as the text color, and add each line on a separate layer. Use a different font size and line spacing settings for each line. If needed, use the Edit, Free Transform (Ctrl/Command+T) command to resize and reposition the text so that it overlaps slightly.

Project 5: Basic Photo Repair

Digital cameras enable you to take quick and easy snapshots without having to fiddle with numerous settings. (You can change settings on most cameras if you prefer not to use an automatic mode.) Sometimes, due to inadequate lighting or focus, the subject of the photograph will appear too dark or blurred. Using Photoshop 7.0's powerful photo correction features, you can convert a picture with improper exposure into a professional-quality image.

Basic Photo Repair

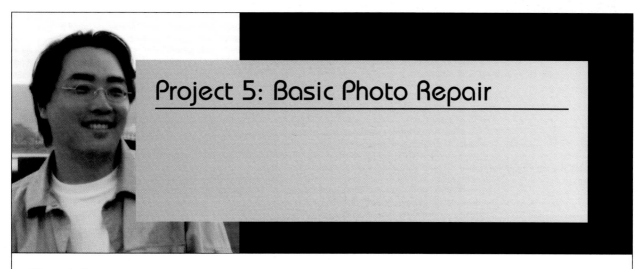

Project 5: Basic Photo Repair

Total Steps

STEP 1.   Correcting the Source Photo's Brightness

STEP 2.   Sharpening the Image

STEP 3.   Adjusting the Image Color

STEP 4.   Removing Grain and Making Additional Color Corrections

STEP 5.   Removing Fine Lines with the Healing Brush

STEP 6.   Restoring the Face

STEP 7.   Starting the Liquify Filter to Reshape the Face

STEP 8.   Reshaping the Cheek and Neck

STEP 9.   Comparing Facial Contours

STEP 10. Copying the Background Layer and Applying Cutout Effects

STEP 11. Adjusting the Colors

STEP 12. Blurring the Copied Layer

STEP 13. Blending the Copied Layer to Complete the Image

STEP 1. Correcting the Source Photo's Brightness

Choose File, Open (Ctrl/Command+O) and open the Book\Sources\smile.jpg file from the supplementary CD-ROM. Because the picture was taken at night without a flash, it's too dark. Choose Image, Adjustments, Levels (Ctrl/Command+L) from the menu bar to open the Levels dialog box. Move the center Input Levels slider to the position shown here, and then click OK to brighten the image.

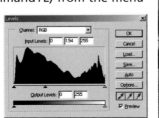

smile.jpg

 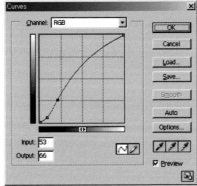

STEP 2. Sharpening the Image

Choose Image, Adjustments, Curves (Ctrl/Command+M) from the menu bar to open the Curves dialog box. In the Curves dialog box, bend the curve into the shape shown here. To do so, click the diagonal line to create points on the curve, and then drag them into position. Click OK to apply the changes and bring the picture into sharper focus.

STEP 3. Adjusting the Image Color

Choose Image, Adjustments, Auto Color to correct the color automatically using the most optimal colors. However, the image still has strong greenish overtones. To correct them, choose Image, Adjustments, Variations to open the Variations dialog box. Click the More Red and More Yellow thumbnails once each, and then click OK to increase orange tones in the image, restoring its color.

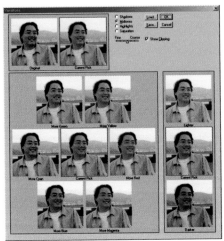

STEP 4. Removing Grain and Making Additional Color Corrections

Some graininess mars the picture. Choose Filter, Noise, Despeckle from the menu bar, and then press Ctrl/Command+F two times to remove the graininess. We will now make the image more yellow in color. Choose Image, Adjustments, Variations to open the Variations dialog box, and then click OK to enhance the image's yellow tones.

STEP 5. Removing Fine Lines with the Healing Brush

Photoshop 7.0's new Healing Brush tool enables you to remove imperfections from an image with ease. Use the Navigator palette to zoom the image to 100% size and center the man's face in the image window. Choose the Healing Brush tool from the toolbar. Alt/Option-click on a rather clean spot in the face to load a repair source for the brush, and then click or drag on the lines and imperfections. (If needed, use the Brush Preset picker to choose alternative brush sizes.) Alt/Option-click additional locations to load repair sources with different color values. Like the Clone Stamp tool, the Healing Brush tool stamps the repair source over the areas specified; in addition, the Healing Brush tool blends the repair with the surrounding colors to provide the most optimal change.

STEP 6. Restoring the Face

Continue to use the Healing Brush tool to remove fine imperfections from the man's face. When you finish, use the Navigator palette to zoom the image back out to 50% size.

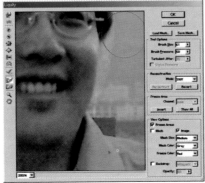

STEP 7. Starting the Liquify Filter to Reshape the Face

Using the Liquify filter, which has been improved for Photoshop 7.0, you can change the contours of the man's face. Choose Filter, Liquify from the menu bar to open the Liquify dialog box. Click the Zoom tool in the toolbox at the left side of the dialog box, and click twice on the man's right cheek to magnify this area. Click the Freeze tool in the toolbox at the left, and drag in the right size of the image preview to apply a mask, shown here in red. The mask protects the areas surrounding the face, so they are not affected by the Liquify filter.

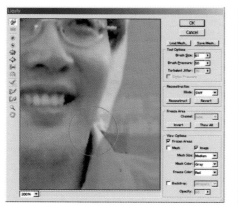 

STEP 9. Comparing Facial Contours

Compare the images before and after applying the Liquify filter. The facial contours look much more attractive in the edited image on the bottom.

STEP 8. Reshaping the Cheek and Neck

Click the Warp tool in the toolbox at the left, and then use the Tool Options settings at the right side of the dialog box to adjust the brush size as shown here. Move the mouse pointer just to the right of the man's right cheek, and then drag left to increase the cheek contour, making the man's face appear thinner. Click the Zoom tool again, and then Alt/Option-click on the image to zoom back out to 100%. Use the Freeze tool to mask off the area to the left of the stray hairs on the left side of the man's head, and then use the Warp tool to push up the hairs to the right. If desired, also mask the man's neck and nape area at the left, and use the Warp tool to push those areas to the right so the man's neck appears thinner. Click OK to apply the Liquify changes.

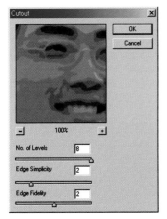

STEP 10. Copying the Background Layer and Applying Cutout Effects

Copy the Background layer by dragging it onto the Create a new layer button on the Layers palette. With the new Background copy layer selected in the Layers palette, choose Filter, Artistic, Cutout from the menu bar to open the Cutout dialog box. Choose the settings shown here, and then click OK to simplify the image colors and shapes.

STEP 11. Adjusting the Colors

With the Background copy layer still selected in the Layers palette, choose Image, Adjustments, Hue/Saturation (Ctrl/Command+U) from the menu bar to open the Hue/Saturation dialog box. Drag the sliders to specify the settings shown here, and then click OK to give the cutout colors a brownish tint.

STEP 12. Blurring the Copied Layer

With the Background copy layer still selected in the Layers palette, choose Filter, Blur, Gaussian Blur from the menu bar to open the Gaussian Blur dialog box. Set the Radius to 4.4, and then click OK to blur the cutout image.

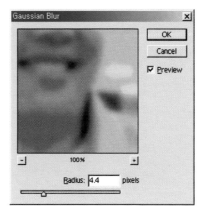

STEP 13. Blending the Copied Layer to Complete the Image

With the Background copy layer still selected in the Layers palette, click the Add a layer style button, and then click Blending Options. Choose Overlay from the Blend Mode drop-down list in the Layer Style dialog box, and then click OK. Then, use the Fill slider on the Layers palette to change the Fill setting for the Background copy layer to 57%, further blending the layers for a fantastic result.

Project 6: Cross Filter Effect

In this project, work with a digital camera image showing a city night view. Emphasizing the glistening street lamps and streets creates an appealing nightlife scene. See how to add a star-shaped filter effect to pump the image up a notch.

Cross Filter Effect

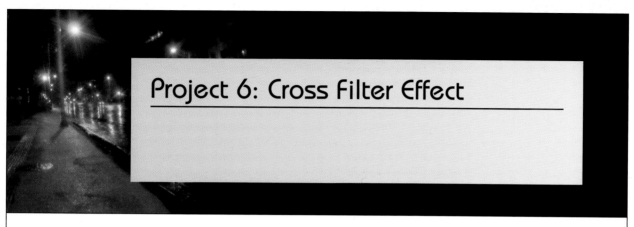

Project 6: Cross Filter Effect

Total Steps

STEP 1.   Zooming the Source Photo
STEP 2.   Measuring the Light's Angle
STEP 3.   Rotating the Image to Change the Light's Angle
STEP 4.   Adding Wind to Diffuse the Light
STEP 5.   Adding and Blending More Wind
STEP 6.   Rotating the Layer and Creating More Wind
STEP 7.   Blending the Diffused Light
STEP 8.   Rotating the Image
STEP 9.   Applying Still More Wind
STEP 10. Completing the Star-Shaped Light Effects
STEP 11. Rotating the Image to its Original Orientation
STEP 12. Blending the Layers
STEP 13. Copying and Blurring the Original Photo Layer
STEP 14. Blending the Blurred Layer
STEP 15. Softening the Light Rays

STEP 1.
Zooming the Source Photo

Choose File, Open (Ctrl/Command+O) and open the Book\Sources\street.jpg file from the supplementary CD-ROM. Choose the Zoom tool from the toolbox, and then drag to select the area that includes the street lamp near the upper-left corner of the image. The image zooms in on the street lamp.

street.jpg

STEP 2. Measuring the Light's Angle

A slanted line of light extends from either side of the street lamp's light. Choose Window, Info to display the Info palette. Then, choose the Measure tool from the toolbox. Drag along the slanted line of light to add a rule line identifying the light's angle. The A value at the top-right side of the Info palette calculates the angle based on the rule you drew. As shown here, the angle is approximately -20°. Click Clear on the Options bar to remove the rule. Choose Window, Navigator to redisplay the Navigator palette, and zoom back out so you can see the whole image in the image window.

STEP 3. Rotating the Image to Change the Light's Angle

Click the Default Foreground and Background Colors button on the toolbox, and then click the Switch Foreground and Background Colors button on the toolbox to set the background color to black. Choose Image, Rotate Canvas, Arbitrary from the menu bar to open the Rotate Canvas dialog box. Enter 20 in the Angle text box, click the CCW option button, and then click OK to rotate the image 20° counterclockwise. The line of light now has horizontal alignment.

STEP 4. Adding Wind to Diffuse the Light

Copy the Background layer by dragging it onto the Create a new layer button on the Layers palette. With the Background copy layer still selected, choose Filter, Stylize, Wind from the menu bar to open the Wind dialog box. Click the From the Left option button, and then click OK to create a wind effect that blows from the left to the right.

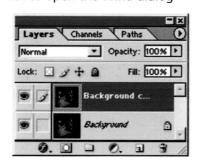

STEP 5. Adding and Blending More Wind

Choose Filter, Stylize, Wind again. Click the From the Right option button in the Wind dialog box, and then click OK. Now the light spreads in both directions. With the Background copy layer still selected in the

Layers palette, click the Add a layer style button, and then click Blending Options. Choose Lighten from the Blend Mode drop-down list in the Layer Style dialog box, change the Fill Opacity setting to 50%, and then click OK to make the horizontal ray of light appear more natural.

STEP 6. Rotating the Image and Creating More Wind

Choose Image, Rotate Canvas, Arbitrary from the menu bar. In the Rotate Canvas dialog box, set the Angle to 60, click the CCW option button, and then click OK to rotate the image 60° counterclockwise. Copy the Background layer by dragging it onto the Create a new layer button on the Layers palette. Move the new Background copy 2 layer to the top of the Layers palette. With the Background copy 2 layer still selected, choose Filter, Stylize, Wind, click From the Left, and then click OK. Choose Filter, Stylize, Wind, click From the Right, then click OK. This adds wind to spread the light in two more directions.

STEP 7. Blending the Diffused Light

With the Background copy 2 layer still selected in the Layers palette, click the Add a layer style button, and then click Blending Options. Choose Lighten from the Blend Mode drop-down list in the Layer Style dialog box, change the Fill Opacity setting to 50%, and then click OK to make the horizontal ray of light appear more natural.

The horizontal rays of light on the layers blend naturally to form an "X."

STEP 8. Rotating the Image

Choose Image, Rotate Canvas, Arbitrary from the menu bar. In the Rotate Canvas dialog box, set the Angle to 60, click the CCW option button, and then click OK to rotate the image 60° counterclockwise.

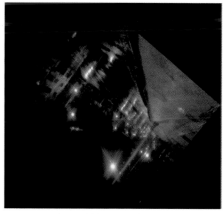

STEP 9. Applying Still More Wind

Copy the Background layer by dragging it onto the Create a new layer button on the Layers palette. Drag the new layer, Background copy 3, to the top of the Layers palette. Choose Filter, Stylize, Wind, click From the Left, and then click OK. Choose Filter, Stylize, Wind, click From the Right, and then click OK. This adds wind to spread the light in two more directions.

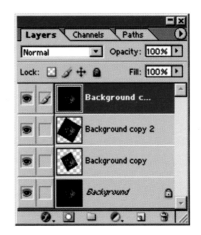

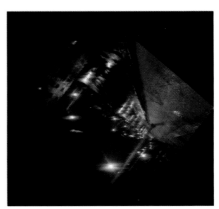

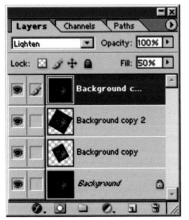

STEP 10. Completing the Star-Shaped Light Effects

With the Background copy 3 layer still selected in the Layers palette, click the Add a layer style button, and then click Blending Options. Choose Lighten from the Blend Mode drop-down list in the Layer Style dialog box, change the Fill Opacity setting to 50%, and then click OK to blend all the rays of light, making each light source in the image appear star-shaped.

STEP 11. Rotating the Image to its Original Orientation

Now, rotate the image back to its original orientation. Because you have rotated the image a total of 140° (20+60+60), rotate the image 220 in the same direction to make one revolution (360°). Choose Image, Rotate Canvas, Arbitrary from the menu bar. In the Rotate Canvas dialog box, set the Angle to 220, click the CCW option button, and then click OK to rotate the image 220° counterclockwise. Because rotating the image caused the canvas size to increase to accommodate the content of the various layers, choose the Crop tool from the toolbox, drag in the image window to select the image itself, and then press Enter/Return to crop out the black area surrounding the image.

STEP 12. Blending the Layers

Click the eye icon beside the Background layer in the Layers palette to hide that layer, leaving the three layers blended with the Lighten mode visible. Click the palette menu button in the upper-right corner of the Layers palette, and click Merge Visible to merge the three layers. Click the eye icon box beside the Background layer to redisplay the layer.

STEP 13. Copying and Blurring the Original Photo Layer

Copy the Background layer by dragging it onto the Create a new layer button on the Layers palette. Drag the new Background copy layer to the top of the Layers palette. Choose Filter, Blur, Gaussian Blur from the menu bar to open the Gaussian Blur dialog box. Set the Radius to 6, and then click OK to blur the contents of the new layer.

STEP 14. Blending the Blurred Layer

With the Background copy layer selected in the Layers palette, click the Add a layer style button, and then click Blending Options. Choose Screen from the Blend Mode drop-down list in the Layer Style dialog box, change the Fill Opacity setting to 50%, and then click OK to blend the softened image with the light rays.

STEP 15. Softening the Light Rays

Click the Background copy 3 layer in the Layers palette. Choose Filter, Blur, Blur More from the menu bar to soften the somewhat sharp star-shaped lights. The star-shaped lights glow on the city streets to create a beautiful image.

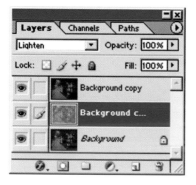

Project 7: Engraving Collage

In this project, convert pictures of people to black and white, and then adjust the image levels to create a silk screen effect. Combine the photos in a single image, use various blend modes, and then add a bluish tone and text to complete the image.

Engraving Collage

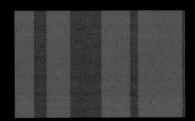

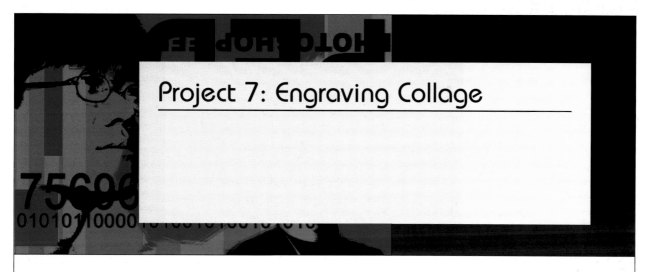

Project 7: Engraving Collage

Total Steps

STEP 1.   Opening the Source Photos

STEP 2.   Making the First Image Black and White

STEP 3.   Making the Second Image Black and White

STEP 4.   Removing the Black Background from the Second Image

STEP 5.   Making the Third Image Black and White

STEP 6.   Removing the Black Background from the Third Image

STEP 7.   Making a New Blue Image

STEP 8.   Selecting Vertical Strips

STEP 9.   Filling the Vertical Strips with Gray

STEP 10. Blending the Gray Strips

STEP 11. Adding Black Rectangles

STEP 12. Blending the Black Rectangles

STEP 13. Blending the Third Image

STEP 14. Rotating the New Layer

STEP 15. Blending the First Image

STEP 16. Blending the Second Image

STEP 17. Adding Black Text to Complete the Image

STEP 1. Opening the Source Photos

Choose File, Open (Ctrl/Command+O) and open the Book\Sources\pic_01.jpg, Book\Sources\pic_02.jpg, and Book\Sources\pic_03.jpg files from the supplementary CD-ROM.

pic_01.jpg   pic_02.jpg   pic_03.jpg

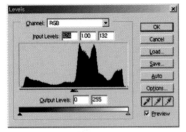

STEP 2. Making the First Image Black and White

Choose Window, Documents, pic_01.jpg to select the first image file. Choose Image, Adjustments, Desaturate (Shift+Ctrl/Command+U) from the menu bar to convert the image to black and white. Choose Image, Adjustments, Levels (Ctrl/Command+L) to open the Levels dialog box. Move the Input Levels sliders toward the center as shown here, and then click OK to eliminate gray tones from the image.

STEP 3. Making the Second Image Black and White

Choose Window, Documents, pic_02.jpg to select the second image file. Choose Image, Adjustments, Desaturate (Shift+Ctrl/Command+U) from the menu bar to convert the image to black and white. Choose Image, Adjustments, Levels (Ctrl/Command+L) to open the Levels dialog box. Move the Input Levels sliders toward the center as shown here, and then click OK to eliminate gray tones from the image. In this case, the background area also turns black.

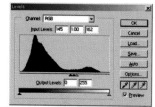

STEP 4.
Removing the Black Background from the Second Image

Choose the Brush tool from the toolbox. Click the Click to open the Brush Preset picker button on the Options bar, and then double-click the Spatter 46 pixels brush type to choose that brush and close the preset picker. Set the foreground color to white, and then use the Brush tool to cover the background with rough white brush strokes. Some black areas show here and there.

STEP 5.
Making the Third Image Black and White

Choose Window, Documents, pic_03.jpg to select the third image file. Choose Image, Adjustments, Desaturate (Shift+Ctrl/Command+U) from the menu bar to convert the image to black and white. Choose Image, Adjustments, Levels (Ctrl/Command+L) to open the Levels dialog box. Move the Input Levels sliders toward the center as shown here, and then click OK to eliminate gray tones from the image.

STEP 6. Removing the Black Background from the Third Image

Choose the Brush tool from the toolbox. With the Spatter 46 pixels brush still selected and the foreground color still set to white, use the Brush tool to cover the background with rough white brush strokes as before. Some black areas show here and there.

STEP 7. Making a New Blue Image

Choose File, New (Ctrl/Command+N) from the menu bar to open the New dialog box. Set the Width to 800 pixels, the Height to 485 pixels, and the Resolution to 150 pixels/inch. Click the White option button under Contents, and then click OK to open the new image window. Use the Color palette to set the foreground color to blue (R:0, G:121, B:255). Use the Paint Bucket tool or press Alt/Option+Del to fill the new image with blue.

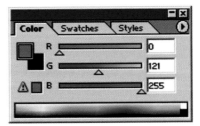

STEP 8. Selecting Vertical Strips

Choose the Rectangular Marquee tool from the toolbox, and select the vertical areas shown here. (After you select the first area, press and hold the Shift key as you make the other selections.)

STEP 9. Filling the Vertical Strips with Gray

Click the Create a new layer button (Shift+Ctrl/Command+N) in the Layers palette to add a new layer named Layer 2. Use the Color palette to set the foreground color to a dark gray (R:125, G:123, B:125), and then use the Paint Bucket tool or press Alt/Option+Del to fill the selection marquee with gray on the new layer. Choose Select, Deselect (Ctrl/Command+D) to remove the selection marquee.

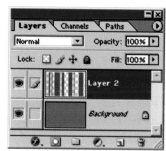

STEP 10. Blending the Gray Strips

With Layer 2 still selected in the Layers palette, click the Add a layer style button, and then click Blending Options. Choose Multiply from the Blend Mode drop-down list in the Layer Style dialog box, change the Fill Opacity setting to 22%, and then click OK. The gray strips blend with the blue background to form lighter and darker strips.

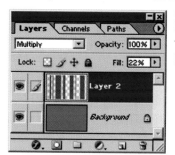

STEP 11. Adding Black Rectangles

Choose the Rectangular Marquee tool from the toolbox, and select the rectangular areas shown here. (After you select the first area, press and hold the Shift key as you make the other selections.) Click the Background layer in the Layers palette, and then click the Create a new layer button (Shift+Ctrl/Command+N) to add a new layer named Layer 3 by default. Click the Default Foreground and Background Colors button on the toolbox to set the foreground color to black, and then use the Paint Bucket tool or press Alt/Option+Del to fill the selection in black on the new layer. Choose Select, Deselect (Ctrl/Command+D) to remove the selection marquee.

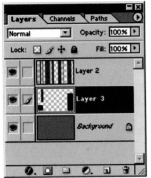

STEP 12. Blending the Black Rectangles

With Layer 3 still selected in the Layers palette, click the Add a layer style button, and then click Blending Options. Choose Color Burn from the Blend Mode drop-down list in the Layer Style dialog box, and then click OK. The black rectangles change to a dark blue and blend with the background.

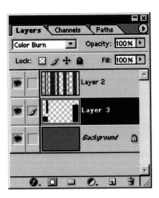

STEP 13. Blending the Third Image

Position image windows so you can see the windows for both the blue image (where you'll be building the collage now) and pic_03.jpg. Choose the Move tool from the toolbox, and then drag from the pic_03.jpg window to the window for the blue image. This copies the picture into a new layer named Layer 4 in the collage image file. Use the Move tool to position the Layer 4 content in the center of the image. Choose Edit, Free Transform (Ctrl/Command+T), drag the handles to resize the man's image as shown here, and then press Enter/Return. With Layer 4 still selected in the Layers palette, click the Add a layer style button, and then click Blending Options. Choose Color Burn from the Blend Mode drop-down list in the Layer Style dialog box, and then click OK. The man's image changes to a dark blue and blends with the background.

STEP 14. Rotating the New Layer

With Layer 4 still selected in the Layers palette, choose Edit, Transform, Rotate 180° from the menu bar. The man's image flips on the layer.

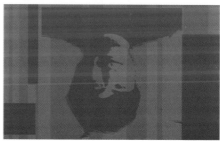

STEP 15. Blending the First Image

Position image windows so you can see the windows for both the collage image and pic_01.jpg. Choose the Move tool from the toolbox, and then drag from the pic_01.jpg window to the window for the blue image. This copies the picture into a new layer named Layer 5 in the collage image file. Use the Move tool to position the Layer 5 content at the left side of the image. Choose Edit, Free Transform (Ctrl/Command+T), drag the handles to resize the man's image as shown here, and then press Enter/Return. With Layer 5 still selected in the Layers palette, click the Add a layer style button, and then click Blending Options. Choose Multiply from the Blend Mode drop-down list in the Layer Style dialog box, and then click OK.

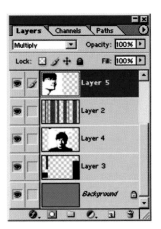

The white areas of the man's image become transparent.

STEP 16. Blending the Second Image

Position image windows so you can see the windows for both the collage image and pic_02.jpg. Choose the Move tool from the toolbox, and then drag from the pic_02.jpg window to the window for the blue image. This copies the picture into a new layer named Layer 6 in the collage image file. Use the Move tool to position the Layer 6 content at the right side of the image. Choose Edit, Free Transform (Ctrl/Command+T), drag the handles to resize the man's image as shown here, and then press Enter/Return. With Layer 6 still selected in the Layers palette, click the Add a layer style button, and then click Blending Options. Choose Multiply from the Blend Mode drop-down list in the Layer Style dialog box, and then click OK.

STEP 17. Adding Black Text to Complete the Image

Use the Horizontal Type tool and the Character palette to add text of various sizes into the image, as shown here. Use the Edit, Transform, Rotate 180° command to flip text on its layer, as needed.

make-up
PED's skincare
PED special
base make-up
hair special
debut model
diet & health

2002 PED*
Pastel **Floral**

Project 8: Nice Close-Up

In this project, work with a picture that was taken at an angle for effect. Correct and crop the image, and then add colored background shapes to create a professional, provocative finished image.

make-up
PED's skincare
PED special
base make-up
hair special
debut model
diet & health

2002 **PED**＊
Pastel **Floral**

Nice Close-Up

Project 8: Nice Close-Up

Pastel **Floral**

Total Steps

STEP 1.   Opening the Source Photo
STEP 2.   Copying and Blurring a Layer
STEP 3.   Blending the Copied Layer
STEP 4.   Merging the Layers
STEP 5.   Darkening the Image
STEP 6.   Using the Healing Brush to Remove Noise
STEP 7.   Continuing to Restore the Woman's Face
STEP 8.   Filling the Right Side of the Image with White
STEP 9.   Copying and Blurring the Layer
STEP 10. Blending the Copied Layer
STEP 11. Copying the Layer and Making a Bright Blend

STEP 12. Copying the Layer and Making a Clear Blend
STEP 13. Adding a Black Shape Layer
STEP 14. Adding a Hole in the Black Shape Layer
STEP 15. Adjusting the Hole's Shape
STEP 16. Adding and Modifying a Circle Shape
STEP 17. Adding Text over the Blue Circle
STEP 18. Selecting a Polygon Shape
STEP 19. Filling and Blending the Shape
STEP 20. Copying and Positioning a New Layer
STEP 21. Copying and Blending another Layer
STEP 22. Adding Text to Complete the Image

STEP 1. Opening the Source Photo

Choose File, Open (Ctrl/Command+O) and open the Book\Sources\closeup.jpg file from the supplementary CD-ROM. Too much lighting was used when the picture was taken, making the overall image blurry, with noise particles here and there.

closeup.jpg

STEP 2. Copying and Blurring a Layer

Copy the Background layer by dragging it onto the Create a new layer button on the Layers palette. With the new Background copy layer selected in the Layers palette, choose Filter, Blur, Gaussian Blur from the menu bar. Set the Radius to 4 in the Gaussian Blur dialog box, and then click OK to blur the layer.

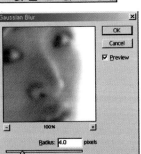

STEP 3. Blending the Copied Layer

With the Background copy layer still selected in the Layers palette, click the Add a layer style button, and then click Blending Options. Choose Soft Light from the Blend Mode drop-down list in the Layer Style dialog box, and then click OK. Copy the Background copy layer by dragging it onto the Create a new layer button on the Layers palette. The addition of the Background copy 2 layer emphasizes the soft light effect.

STEP 4. Merging the Layers

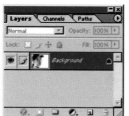

Click the palette menu button in the upper-right corner of the Layers palette, and then click Flatten Image to merge all the layers into the Background layer.

STEP 5. Darkening the Image

Choose Image, Adjustments, Levels (Ctrl/Command+L) from the menu bar to open the Levels dialog box. Drag the right Output Levels slider to the left as shown here, and then click OK to darken the image overall. This step prevents the face from becoming too pale when you later apply blend modes.

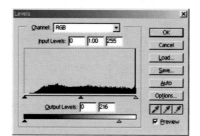

STEP 6. Using the Healing Brush to Remove Noise

Next, remove the noise from the woman's face. Choose the Healing Brush tool from the toolbox. Use the Brush Preset picker on the Options bar to choose another brush size, if desired. Alt/Option-click on a clean area of skin on the right cheek to specify the repair source for the tool. Click the blotches on the chin to remove them.

STEP 7. Continuing to Restore the Woman's Face

Alt/Option-click as needed to choose additional repair sources, and then click to apply the repair with the Healing Brush tool. Continue until you remove all blotches and fine lines from the woman's face.

STEP 9. Copying and Blurring the Layer

Copy the Background layer by dragging it onto the Create a new layer button on the Layers palette. With the new Background copy layer still selected, choose Filter, Blur, Gaussian Blur from the menu bar. Change the Radius to 4.2 in the Gaussian Blur dialog box, and then click OK to blur the layer.

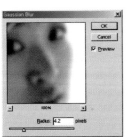 

STEP 8. Filling the Right Side of the Image with White

Choose the Magic Wand tool from the toolbox, and change the Tolerance setting on the Options bar to 3. Click the gray area to the right of the woman's face to select the right side of the image. Click the Default Foreground and Background Colors button on the toolbox to set the background color to white, and then press Del to remove the selection contents, leaving a white area at the right side of the image and sharpening the edge of the woman's face. Choose Select, Deselect (Ctrl/Command+D) to remove the selection marquee.

STEP 10. Blending the Copied Layer

With the Background copy layer still selected in the Layers palette, click the Add a layer style button, and then click

Blending Options. Choose Overlay from the Blend Mode drop-down list in the Layer Style dialog box, and then click OK to emphasize the shading in the image. However, this step makes the image too dark.

STEP 11. Copying the Layer and Making a Bright Blend

Copy the Background copy layer by dragging it onto the Create a new layer button in the Layers palette. With the new Background copy 2 layer still selected in the Layers palette, click the Add a layer style button, and then click Blending Options. Choose Screen from the Blend Mode drop-down list in the Layer Style dialog box, and then click OK to brighten up the image.

STEP 12. Copying the Layer and Making a Clear Blend

Copy the Background layer by dragging it onto the Create a new layer button on the Layers palette. With the new Background copy 3 layer still selected in the Layers palette, click the Add a layer style button, and then click Blending Options. Choose Overlay from the Blend Mode drop-down list in the Layer Style dialog box, change the Fill Opacity setting to 54%, and then click OK to emphasize the colors in the image.

STEP 13.
Adding a Black Shape Layer

Choose the Rectangle tool from the toolbox, and click the Shape layers button on

 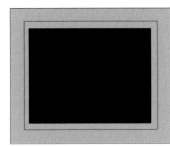

the Options bar. Click the Default Foreground and Background Colors button on the toolbox to set the foreground color to black. Resize the image window and use the Navigator palette to zoom out the image, so gray work area appears around the image in the image window. Drag to make a black rectangle large enough to cover the image. Drag the new shape layer, named Shape 1 by default, to the top of the Layers palette.

STEP 14. Adding a Hole in the Black Shape Layer

With the Rectangle tool still selected, click the Subtract from shape area button on the Options bar. Drag to create a rectangle at the left, approximately over the woman's face, to remove that area from the black layer so the woman's face shows through.

STEP 15. Adjusting the Hole's Shape

Choose the Path Selection tool from the toolbox, and then click on the rectangular hole to display selection handles around it. Choose Edit, Free Transform (Ctrl/Command+T) from the menu bar. Adjust the slant, size, and position of the hole as shown here, and then press Enter/Return to finish the transformation.

STEP 16. Adding and Modifying a Circle Shape

Choose the Ellipse Tool from the toolbar. Make sure that the Shape layers and Create new shape layer buttons are selected on the Options bar. Use the Color palette to set the foreground color to a dark navy blue (R:0,

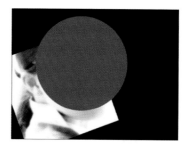

G:0, B:160). Press and hold the Shift key while dragging in the image window to create a circle as shown here. The circle appears on its own new shape layer, named Shape 2 by default. In the Layers palette, Alt/Option-click the border between the two shape layers to group the layers together, so that the area where the hole overlaps the circle is cut from the circular shape.

STEP 17. Adding Text over the Blue Circle

Choose the Horizontal Type tool from the toolbox. Click the Toggle the Character and Paragraph palettes button on the Options bar to open the Character palette, and then specify the text settings shown here. Type all the text shown here on a single layer, pressing Enter to start each new line, and pressing the Space bar multiple times at the beginning of each line to position the text according to the slant of the image. Select "PED special," and change the Color setting to white in the Character palette. Finally, click the Commit any current edits button at the right end of the Options bar to finish adding the text.

STEP 18. Selecting a Polygon Shape

Choose the Polygonal Lasso tool from the toolbox, and use it to make a selection as shown here.

STEP 19. Filling and Blending the Shape

Click the Create a new layer button (Shift+Ctrl/Command +N) on the Layers palette to add a new layer named Layer 1 by default. Use the Color palette to set

the foreground color to a light blue, and then use the Paint Bucket tool or press Alt/Option+Del to fill the selection with blue on the new layer. With Layer 1 still selected in the Layers palette, click the Add a layer style button, and then click Blending Options. Choose Hard Light from the Blend Mode drop-down list in the Layer Style dialog box, and then click OK to darken the shape's blue tone. Choose Select, Deselect (Ctrl/Command+D) to remove the selection marquee.

STEP 20. Copying and Positioning a New Layer

Drag Layer 1 onto the Create a new

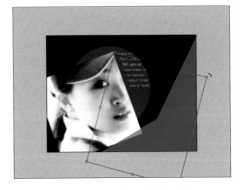

layer button on the Layers palette to create a copy of the layer named Layer 1 copy. Choose Edit, Free Transform (Ctrl/Command+T) from the menu bar,

use the handles that appear to rotate and position the shape on the duplicate layer as shown here, and then press Enter/Return.

STEP 21. Copying and Blending another Layer

Drag Layer 1 copy onto the Create a new layer button on the Layers palette to create a copy of the layer named Layer 1 copy 2. Choose Edit, Free Transform (Ctrl/Command+T) from the menu bar, use the handles that appear to rotate and position the shape on the duplicate layer as shown here, and then press Enter/Return. With Layer 1 copy 2 still selected in the Layers palette, click the Add a layer style button, and then click Blending Options. Choose Lighten from the Blend Mode drop-down list in the Layer Style dialog box, and then click OK to lighten the blue tone of the shape on the layer.

STEP 22. Adding Text to Complete the Image

Use the Horizontal Type tool and the Character palette to add the remaining text shown in the lower-left corner of the image. The bright photo contrasts with the dark background to create a strong image for Web or magazine use.

Project 9: Creative Artwork

In this project, take an old portrait and transform it into a work of art. Emphasize the details in the picture and effectively apply color to the darker regions of the image. Overlap and blend textures made or taken from various picture sources to complete this homage to the demonstrator who set himself on fire in the name of independence.

Creative Artwork

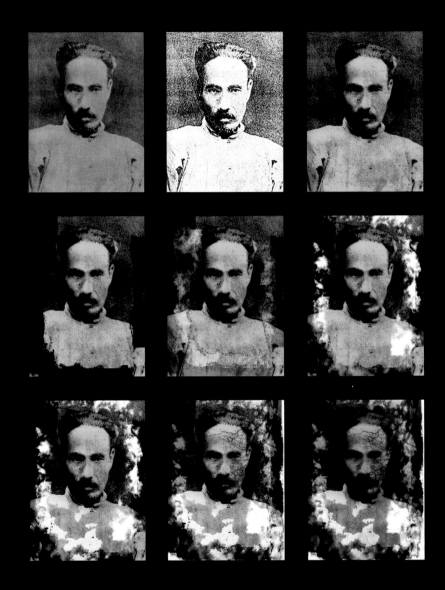

Project 9: Creative Artwork

Total Steps

STEP 1. Resizing the Source Photo
STEP 2. Copying the Layer and Removing Noise
STEP 3. Lightening the Image
STEP 4. Copying a Layer and Emphasizing the Tones
STEP 5. Adjusting Image Brightness
STEP 6. Blending the Background Copy 2 Layer
STEP 7. Copying and Smudging a Layer
STEP 8. Blending the Smudged Layer
STEP 9. Colorizing the Background Copy 3 Layer
STEP 10. Colorizing the Background Copy 2 Layer
STEP 11. Colorizing the Background Copy Layer
STEP 12. Adding Black Borders
STEP 13. Adding Texture to the Black Borders
STEP 14. Blending the Black Borders
STEP 15. Adding White Borders
STEP 16. Adding Texture to the White Borders
STEP 17. Emphasizing the Black Borders

STEP 18. Adding a Cloud Texture Layer
STEP 19. Converting the Clouds to Ink Blots
STEP 20. Adjusting the Texture's Gray Tones
STEP 21. Inverting and Resizing the Texture
STEP 22. Blurring the Texture
STEP 23. Blending the Texture
STEP 24. Colorizing the Texture Layer
STEP 25. Choosing a Flower Brush
STEP 26. Making a Bouquet of Flowers on a New Layer
STEP 27. Blending the Bouquet
STEP 28. Importing the Tree Image
STEP 29. Arranging and Blending the Tree Image
STEP 30. Restoring the Color of the Background Copy Layer
STEP 31. Restoring the Color of the Background Copy 2 Layer
STEP 32. Restoring the Color of the Background Copy 3 Layer
STEP 33. Blending the Black Borders
STEP 34. Adjusting the Bouquet Color to Complete the Image

STEP 1. Resizing the Source Photo

Choose File, Open (Ctrl/Command+O) and open the Book\Sources\portrait.jpg file from the supplementary CD-ROM. Due to the portrait's age, noise covers it and the overall size is very small. Choose Image, Image Size from the menu bar to open the Image Size dialog box. In the Pixel Dimensions area of the dialog box, enter 300 in the Width text box and choose percent from the Width drop-down list. Make sure the Height settings also change to 300 percent, and then click OK to increase the image's size by 300%. Use the Navigator palette to zoom the image to 25%, so you can see the full image onscreen. Finally, choose Image, Mode, RGB color to change the image to the RGB color mode, even though it still appears black and white.

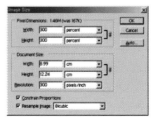

portrait.jpg

STEP 2. Copying the Layer and Removing Noise

Copy the Background layer by dragging it onto the Create a new layer button on the Layers palette. With the new Background copy layer selected, choose Filter, Noise, Median from the menu bar. Change the Radius to 17 in the Median dialog box, and then click OK to remove the noise and simplify the image.

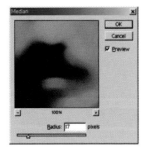

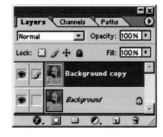

STEP 3. Lightening the Image

Choose Image, Adjustments, Levels (Ctrl/Command+L) from the menu bar to open the Levels dialog box. Drag the center Input Levels slider to the position shown here, and then click OK to lighten the image overall.

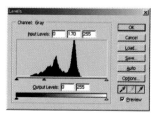

STEP 4. Copying a Layer and Emphasizing the Tones

Copy the Background layer by dragging it onto the Create a new layer button on the Layers palette. Drag the new Background copy 2 layer to the top of the Layers palette. With the Background copy 2 layer still selected, choose Filter, Sharpen, Unsharpen Mask from the menu bar. Choose the settings shown here in the Unsharp Mask dialog box, and then click OK to emphasize the dark and light tones in the image.

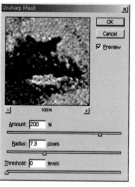

STEP 5. Adjusting Image Brightness

Choose Image, Adjustments, Curves (Ctrl/Command+M) from the menu bar. In the Curves dialog box, bend the curve into the shape shown here. To do so, click the diagonal line to create points on the curve, and then drag them into position. Click OK to apply the changes and lighten the image and emphasize the lights and darks even further.

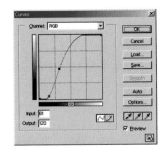

STEP 6. Blending the Background Copy 2 Layer

With the Background copy 2 layer still selected in the Layers palette, click the Add a layer style button, and then click Blending Options. Choose Darken from the Blend Mode drop-down list in the Layer Style dialog box, and then click OK. Only the black pixels in the current layer appear over the image from the layer below.

STEP 7. Copying and Smudging a Layer

Copy the Background layer by dragging it onto the Create a new layer button on the Layers palette. Drag the new Background copy 3 layer to the top of the Layers palette. With the new layer still selected, choose Filter, Artistic, Smudge Stick from the menu bar. Choose the settings shown here in the Smudge Stick dialog box, and make the following configurations to make it appear as if the image were drawn by hand using a short piece of charcoal.

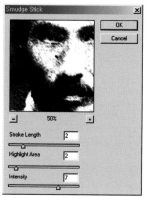

STEP 8. Blending the Smudged Layer

With the Background copy 3 layer still selected in the Layers palette, click the Add a layer style button, and then click Blending Options. Choose Linear Light from the Blend Mode drop-down list in the Layer Style dialog box, change the Fill Opacity setting to 33%, and then click OK to create a strong blend between the layers.

STEP 9. Colorizing the Background Copy 3 Layer

With the Background copy 3 layer selected in the Layers palette, choose Image, Adjustments, Hue/Saturation (Ctrl/Command+U) from the menu bar. In the Hue/Saturation dialog box, click the Colorize check box to check it, drag the sliders to specify the settings shown here, and then click OK to add a purple tone to the Background copy 3 layer.

STEP 10. Colorizing the Background Copy 2 Layer

Click the Background copy 2 layer in the Layers palette. Choose Image, Adjustments, Hue/Saturation (Ctrl/Command+U) from the menu bar. In the Hue/Saturation dialog box, click the Colorize check box to check it, drag the sliders to specify the settings shown here, and then click OK to add a blue tone to the Background copy 2 layer.

STEP 11. Colorizing the Background Copy Layer

Click the Background copy layer in the Layers palette. Choose Image, Adjustments, Hue/Saturation (Ctrl/Command+U) from the menu bar. In the Hue/Saturation dialog box, click the Colorize check box to check it, drag the sliders to specify the settings shown here, and then click OK to add a brown tone to the Background copy layer.

STEP 12.
Adding Black Borders

Choose the Rectangular Marquee tool from the toolbox, and select the rectangular shapes shown here. (After you select the first area, press and hold the Shift key as you make additional selections.) Click the

Create a new layer button (Shift+Ctrl/Command+N) on the Layers palette to add a new layer named Layer 1, and then drag the new layer to the top of the Layers palette. Click the Default Foreground and Background Colors button on the toolbox to set the foreground color to black, and then use the Paint Bucket tool or press Alt/Option+Del to fill the selection with black on Layer 1. Choose Select, Deselect (Ctrl/Command+D) to remove the selection marquee.

STEP 13. Adding Texture to the Black Borders

With the Layer 1 layer still selected in the Layers palette, choose Filter, Distort, Displace from the menu bar. Set both Scale values to 30% in the Displace dialog box, and then click OK. In the Choose a displacement map dialog box that appears, select the Book\Sources\Displace.psd file from the supplementary CD-ROM, and then click Open to use that file as the displace map. The borders take on the rough appearance of chalk strokes.

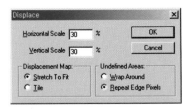

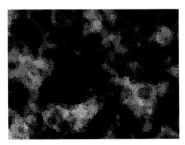

STEP 14. Blending the Black Borders

With the Layer 1 layer still selected in the Layers palette, click the Add a layer style button, and then click Blending Options. Choose Soft Light from the Blend Mode drop-down list in the Layer Style dialog box, and then click OK to blend the borders into the image.

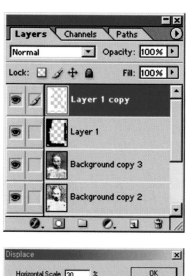

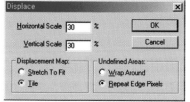

STEP 15. Adding White Borders

Copy Layer 1 by dragging it onto the Create a new layer button on the Layers palette. Choose Layer, Layer Style, Clear Layer Style from the menu bar to remove the Soft Light blending style from the new Layer 1 copy layer. With the new layer still selected, choose Image, Adjustments, Invert (Ctrl/Command+I) from the menu bar. The color on the layer inverts, making the black border white. Choose Edit, Free Transform (Ctrl/Command+T), resize the borders as shown here, and then press Enter/Return. Choose Filter, Distort, Displace from the menu bar. Set both Scale values to 30% in the Displace dialog box, click on Tile under Displacement Map, and then click OK. In the Choose a displacement map dialog box that appears, select the Book\Sources\Displace.psd file from the supplementary CD-ROM, and then click Open to use that file as the displace map. The smaller white borders take on an even rougher appearance.

STEP 16. Adding Texture to the White Borders

With the Layer 1 copy layer still selected in the Layers palette, choose Filter, Render, Difference Clouds from the menu bar. A black and white texture appears in the white border. Press Ctrl/Command+F again as needed to reapply the Difference Clouds filter until the texture reaches the desired appearance. Choose Image, Adjustments, Curves (Ctrl/Command+M) from the menu bar. In the Curves dialog box, bend the curve into the shape shown here. To do so, click the diagonal line to create points on the curve, and then drag them into position. Click OK to apply the changes and emphasize the whites in the texture. Choose Edit, Transform, Rotate 180° to flip the white border. With the Layer 1 copy layer still selected in the Layers palette, click the Add a layer style button, and then click Blending Options. Choose Linear Dodge from the Blend Mode drop-down list in the Layer Style dialog box, change the Fill Opacity setting to 60%, and then click OK to blend the borders into the image.

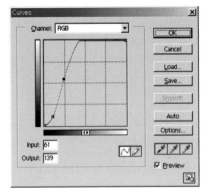

STEP 17. Emphasizing the Black Borders

Click the Layer 1 layer in the Layers palette. Open the Layer Style drop-down list in the upper-left corner of the Layers palette, and then click Color Burn to intensify the blurred black borders.

STEP 18. Adding a Cloud Texture Layer

Click the Create a new layer button (Shift+Ctrl/Command+N) on the Layers palette to add a new layer named Layer 2 by default. Drag the Layer 2 layer to the top of the Layers palette, and then click the eye icon beside each of the other layers in the image to hide them all. With the Layer 2 layer still selected, choose Filter, Render, Clouds from the menu bar to fill the layer with a black and white cloud texture.

 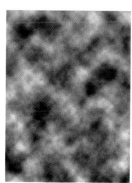

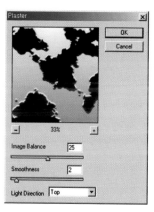 

STEP 19. Converting the Clouds to Ink Blots

Choose Filter, Sketch, Plaster from the menu bar to open the Plaster dialog box. Choose the settings shown here, and then click OK to make the black areas in the texture appear like raised inkblots.

STEP 20. Adjusting the Texture's Gray Tones

With the Layer 2 layer still selected in the Layers palette, choose Image, Adjustments, Curves (Ctrl/Command+M). In the Curves dialog box, bend the curve into the shape shown here. To do so, click the diagonal line to create points on the curve, and then drag them into position. Click OK to apply the changes and evenly distribute the gray background tones on the layer.

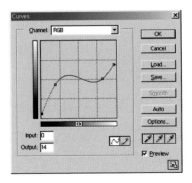

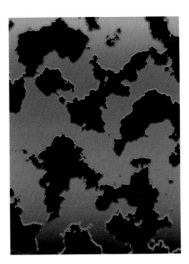

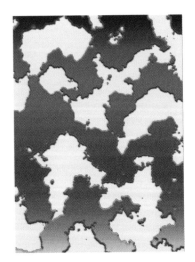

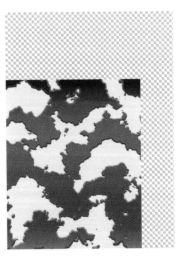

STEP 21. Inverting and Resizing the Texture

Choose Image, Adjustments, Invert (Ctrl/Command+I) from the menu bar to invert the texture's color. Then, choose Edit, Free Transform (Ctrl/Command+T), drag the upper-right handle to reduce the texture image's size as shown here, and then press Enter/Return to finish the transformation.

STEP 22. Blurring the Texture

With the Layer 2 layer still selected, click the Add layer mask button on the Layers palette to apply a mask to the layer. Click the Switch Foreground and Background Colors button on the toolbox to set the foreground color to black and the background color to white. Choose the Gradient tool, and then click the Linear Gradient button on the Options bar. Drag from the upper-right corner of the reduced texture image to its center. The black areas of the gradient identify the transparent areas of the layer mask, creating graduated transparency in the texture.

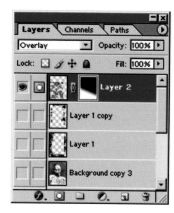

STEP 23. Blending the Texture

Click the eye icon box beside each hidden layer in the Layers palette to view all the layers. With the Layer 2 layer still selected in the palette, open the Layer Style drop-down list in the upper-left corner of the Layers palette, and then click Overlay to add the mottled texture to the image.

STEP 24. Colorizing the Texture Layer

In the Layers palette, click the Layer thumbnail for the Layer 2 layer to enable you to make changes to the layer contents (rather than the mask). Choose Image, Adjustments, Hue/Saturation (Ctrl/Command+U) from the menu bar to open the Hue/Saturation dialog box. Click the Colorize check box to check it, drag the sliders to specify the settings shown here, and then click OK to add a yellow tint to the texture layer.

STEP 25. Choosing a Flower Brush

Choose the Brush tool from the toolbox. Click the Click to open the Brush Preset picker button on the Options bar, and then click the palette menu button in the upper-right corner of the Brush Preset picker. Click Special Effect Brushes in the menu, and then click OK to replace the default brushes in the picker with the special effect brushes. (Choose Reset Brushes from the palette menu at any later time to return to the default brushes.) Click the first brush in the palette (the Azalea brush), drag the Master Diameter slider to set the brush size to 100 px, and then click the Click to open the Brush Preset picker button on the Options bar to close the preset picker.

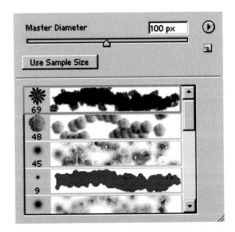

STEP 26. Making a Bouquet of Flowers on a New Layer

Click the Create a new layer button (Shift+Ctrl/Command+N) on the Layers palette to add a new layer named Layer 3. Click or drag in the lower-right corner of the image to add a bouquet of flowers. Choose Image, Adjustments, Hue/Saturation (Ctrl/Command+U) to open the Hue/Saturation dialog box. Click the Colorize check box to check it, drag the sliders to specify the settings shown here, and then click OK to change the color of the flowers to yellow.

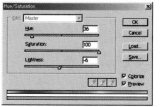

STEP 27. Blending the Bouquet

With the Layer 3 layer still selected in the Layers palette, open the Layer Style drop-down list in the upper-left corner of the Layers palette, and then click Color Dodge to blend the flowers with other elements of the image.

STEP 28. Importing the Tree Image

Choose File, Open (Ctrl/Command+O) and open the Book\Sources\tree.jpg file from the supplementary CD-ROM. Choose the Move tool from the toolbox, and then drag from the tree image window to the image window for this project's file to place a copy of the tree on its own layer in the project file. Use the Move tool to drag the tree on its layer (Layer 4) to the approximate position shown here.

STEP 29. Arranging and Blending the Tree Image

With Layer 4 still selected in the Layers palette, choose Edit, Free Transform (Ctrl/Command+T) from the menu bar. Use the handles that appear to rotate the tree image 180°, drag it to the upper-right corner of the layer, and increase its size. Press Enter/Return to finish the transformation. Open the layer style drop-down list in the upper-left corner of the Layers palette, and then click Linear Burn. Also use the Fill slider on the Layers palette to change the Fill setting to 33% for Layer 4. Now, the white areas of the tree have become transparent, and the black regions blend into the image.

STEP 30. Restoring the Color of the Background Copy Layer

In the Layers palette, right/Control-click the eye icon beside the Background copy layer and then click Show/Hide all other layers in the menu that appears to hide all layers except the Background copy layer. Click the Background copy layer to select it, and then choose Image, Adjustments, Curves (Ctrl/Command+M) from the menu bar. In the Curves dialog box, bend the curve into the shape shown here. To do so, click the diagonal line to create points on the curve, and then drag them into position. Click OK to apply the changes and strengthen the layer's colors.

STEP 31. Restoring the Color of the Background Copy 2 Layer

Click the Background copy 2 layer in the Layers palette to both redisplay and select the layer. Choose Image, Adjustments, Hue/Saturation (Ctrl/Command+U) from the menu bar. In the Hue/Saturation dialog box, drag the Hue slider to choose the setting shown here, and then click OK to apply the changes. The two image layers blend more naturally.

STEP 32. Restoring the Color of the Background Copy 3 Layer

Click the Background copy 3 layer in the Layers palette to both redisplay and select the layer. Choose Image, Adjustments, Curves (Ctrl/Command+M) from the menu bar. In the Curves dialog box, bend the curve into the shape shown

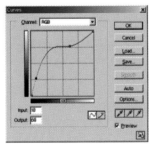

here. To do so, click the diagonal line to create points on the curve, and then drag them into position. Click OK to apply the changes and invert the colors in the dark areas of the image to brighten the image. The three layers combine to create a richer image. The purple hue in the Background copy 2 layer adds dimension to the image.

STEP 33. Blending the Black Borders

Click the Layer 1 layer in the Layers palette to both redisplay and select the layer. Choose Filter, Render, Difference Clouds. Open the Layer Style drop-down list in the upper-left corner of the Layers palette, and then click Multiply. Use the Fill slider on the Layers palette to change the Fill setting for Layer 1 to 94%.

STEP 34. Adjusting the Bouquet Color to Complete the Image

Click the Layer 3 layer in the Layers palette to both redisplay and select the layer. Choose Image, Adjustments, Hue/Saturation (Ctrl/Command+U) from the menu bar to open the Hue/Saturation dialog box. Drag the Saturation slider to choose the setting shown here, and then click OK to blend the prominent flowers into the image. Click the Create a new layer button (Shift+Ctrl/Command+N) on the Layers palette to add a new layer named Layer 5, and drag the layer to the top of the Layers palette. Choose the Lasso tool from the toolbox, select a narrow border area along the right side and in the lower-left corner (pressing Shift to make this second selection) of the layer. With the Layer 5 layer still selected in the Layers palette, choose Filter, Distort, Displace from the menu bar. Set both Scale values to 30% in the Displace dialog box, and then click OK. In the Choose a displacement map dialog box that appears, select the Book\Sources\Displace.psd file from the supplementary CD-ROM, and then click Open to use that file as the displace map. Click the Add a layer style button on the Layers palette, click Inner Shadow, and then click OK in the Layer Style dialog box. Click the eye icon box beside any hidden layers in the Layers palette to redisplay all the layers and verify the resulting composition.

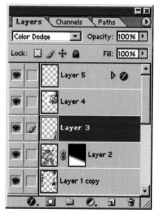

Project 10: Photo Collage

Take a digital picture of a little boy and combine it with
content from various source images to create the cute angel
image shown here. In this project, learn simple techniques to
select and copy the parts you need from various pictures, as
well as blend the parts naturally.

Photo Collage

Project 10: Photo Collage

Total Steps

STEP 1. Opening the Source Photo
STEP 2. Copying a Layer and Correcting the Color
STEP 3. Copying a Layer and Sharpening the Contours
STEP 4. Blending the Sharpened Layer
STEP 5. Copying a Layer and Applying Cutout Effects
STEP 6. Blurring and Blending the Cutout Image
STEP 7. Correcting the Image Color
STEP 8. Removing Noise
STEP 9. Merging the Layers
STEP 10. Starting to Extract the Boy's Head
STEP 11. Extracting the Boy
STEP 12. Selecting the Left Hand in the Second Source Photo
STEP 13. Copying the Left Hand
STEP 14. Selecting the Right Hand in the Third Source Photo
STEP 15. Copying the Right Hand
STEP 16. Selecting the T-Shirt in the Fourth Source Photo
STEP 17. Copying the T-Shirt
STEP 18. Correcting the T-Shirt
STEP 19. Selecting the Harp Image's Background
STEP 20. Selecting the Shadow in Quick Mask Mode
STEP 21. Exiting from the Quick Mask Mode and Copying Only the Harp Image
STEP 22. Making a New Blue Image
STEP 23. Importing and Arranging Each Source Object
STEP 24. Renaming the Layers
STEP 25. Correcting the Color of Both Hands
STEP 26. Matching the Color of the Hands
STEP 27. Making the T-Shirt Black and White
STEP 28. Lightening the T-Shirt
STEP 29. Applying a Blue Tone to the T-Shirt

STEP 30. Adjusting the Harp's Color
STEP 31. Tinting the Harp Brown
STEP 32. Filling in the Space in the Neck
STEP 33. Blurring the Edges of the T-Shirt
STEP 34. Adjusting the Harp's Layer Position
STEP 35. Making a Selection in the Shape of the Right Hand
STEP 36. Removing the Area of the Harp that Hides the Fingers
STEP 37. Applying a Shadow to the Harp Layer
STEP 38. Blurring the Harp Image
STEP 39. Copying the Shadow to another Layer
STEP 40. Softening the Edges of Both Hands
STEP 41. Rotating the Boy
STEP 42. Selecting the Wing
STEP 43. Adding the Wing to the Project
STEP 44. Making the Other Wing
STEP 45. Viewing the Completed Angel
STEP 46. Opening the Flower Image
STEP 47. Starting to Extract the Flower
STEP 48. Extracting the Flower
STEP 49. Copying and Sizing the Flower
STEP 50. Saving the Flower as a Brush
STEP 51. Adjusting the Brush
STEP 52. Adding Flowers with the Flower Brush
STEP 53. Removing the White Background from the Flower Layer
STEP 54. Tinting the Flower Layer Red
STEP 55. Adding Yellow to the Flower Layer
STEP 56. Applying Shadows to the Flower Layer
STEP 57. Adding Text to Complete the Image
STEP 58. Rearranging to a Wide Layout

STEP 1. Opening the Source Photo

Choose File, Open (Ctrl/Command+O) and open the Book\Sources\boy_01.jpg file from the supplementary CD-ROM. This picture was taken late in the day, so you need to correct the dark color before using it in the collage.

boy_01.jpg

STEP 2. Copying the Layer and Correcting the Color

Copy the Background layer by dragging it onto the Create a new layer button on the Layers palette. With the new Background copy layer selected in the Layers palette, choose Image, Adjustments, Auto Color from the menu bar. The Auto Color feature corrects the color, removing the late-day bluish tones from the image.

STEP 3. Copying the Layer and Sharpening the Contours

Copy the Background copy layer by dragging it onto the Create a new layer button on the Layers palette. With the new Background copy 2 layer selected in the Layers palette, choose Filter, Sharpen, Unsharp Mask from the menu bar. Choose the settings shown here in the Unsharp Mask dialog box, and then click OK. Although applying the Unsharp Mask filter removes fuzziness from the image, some pixels of color appear bunched or uneven.

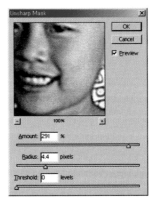

STEP 4. Blending the Sharpened Layer

With the Background copy 2 layer still selected in the Layers palette, open the Layer Style drop-down list in the upper-left corner of the Layers palette, and then click Darken to intensify the dark areas in the current layer (which help sharpen the image) and blend those dark areas with the layer below to create a sharper image.

STEP 5. Copying a Layer and Applying Cutout Effects

Copy the Background copy layer by dragging it onto the Create a new layer button on the Layers palette. Drag the new Background copy 3 layer to the top of the Layers palette. With the new Background copy 3 layer still selected in the Layers palette, choose Filter, Artistic, Cutout from the menu bar. Choose the

settings shown here in the Cutout dialog box, and then click OK to simplify the image into planes of color.

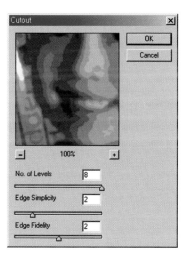

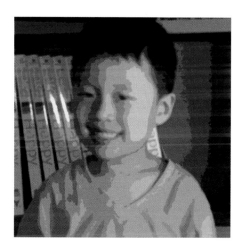

STEP 6. Blurring and Blending the Cutout Image

With the Background copy 3 layer still selected in the Layers palette, choose Filter, Blur, Gaussian Blur from the menu bar. Set the Radius to 4.7 in the Gaussian Blur dialog box, and then click OK to soften color planes. Open the Layer Style drop-down list in the upper-left corner of the Layers palette, and then click Overlay to blend the Background copy 3 layer.

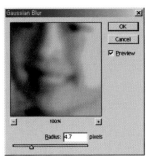

STEP 7. Correcting the Image Color

Choose Image, Adjustments, Variations from the menu bar to open the Variations dialog box. Click the More Red and More Yellow image thumbnails once each, and then click OK to add a warm orange color to the image.

STEP 8. Removing Noise

The darker areas of the image still have too many speckles, or noise particles. Click the Background copy 2 layer in the Layers palette, and then choose Filter, Noise, Median from the menu bar. Change the Radius to 2 in the Median dialog box, and then click OK to reduce the noise.

  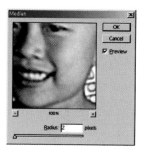

STEP 9. Merging the Layers

Click the palette menu button in the upper-right corner of the Layers palette, and then click Flatten Image to merge all the layers into the Background layer. Choose Image, Adjustments, Levels (Ctrl/Command+L) from the menu bar to open the Levels dialog box. Move the center Input Levels slider to the position shown here, and then click OK to brighten the image color.

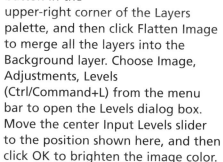

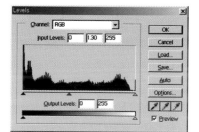

STEP 10. Starting to Extract the Boy's Head

You only need the image of the boy's head for this project. You can use the Extract command to select the areas you need. Choose Filter, Extract from the menu bar to open the Extract dialog box. Click the Edge Highlighter tool in the toolbox at the left side of the dialog box, and highlight the boy's head. Click the Fill tool in the toolbox at the left side of the dialog box, and then click inside of the highlighted edge to specify the selected area.

STEP 11. Extracting the Boy

Click the Preview button in the Extract dialog box to view the area selected for extraction. Chances are, there will be areas where the selection is not as neat as you'd like. Click the Edge Touchup tool in the toolbox at the left side of the Extract dialog box, and then drag along the edges of the image to make the selection neater. Also click the Cleanup tool in the toolbox and drag that tool over the messy areas to clean them up. Finally, click the OK button to complete the extraction, neatly removing all parts of the image that were not part of the selection.

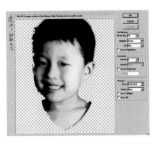
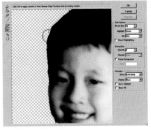

STEP 12. Selecting the Left Hand in the Second Source Photo

You will copy the boy's two hands from two different source images. Choose File, Open (Ctrl/Command+O) and open the Book\Sources\boy_02.jpg file from the supplementary CD-ROM. Choose the Magnetic Lasso tool from the toolbox, and then use it to select only the boy's left hand. Use the Navigator palette to zoom in on the image if that helps you make a more accurate selection.

boy_02.jpg

STEP 13. Copying the Left Hand

Press Ctrl/Command+C to copy the selected hand, and then press Ctrl/Command+V to paste the hand into a new layer named Layer 1 in the image file. Drag the Background layer onto the Delete layer button on the Layers palette to delete the Background layer.

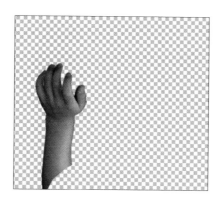

STEP 15. Copying the Right Hand

Press Ctrl/Command+C to copy the selected hand, and then press Ctrl/Command+V to paste the hand into a new layer named Layer 1 in the image file. Drag the Background layer onto the Delete layer button on the Layers palette to delete the Background layer.

STEP 14. Selecting the Right Hand in the Third Source Photo

Choose File, Open (Ctrl/Command+O) and open the Book\Sources\boy_03.jpg file from the supplementary CD-ROM. Choose the Magnetic Lasso tool from the toolbox, and then use it to select only the boy's right hand. Use the Navigator palette to zoom in on the image if that helps you make a more accurate selection.

boy_03.jpg

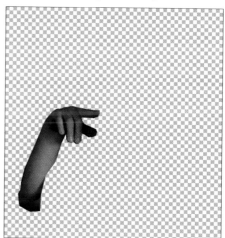

STEP 16. Selecting the T-Shirt in the Fourth Source Photo

Choose File, Open (Ctrl/Command+O) and open the Book\Sources\boy_04.jpg file from the supplementary CD-ROM. Choose the Polygonal Lasso tool from the toolbox, and then use it to select only the boy's orange T-shirt. The boy's face covers the left shoulder of the T-shirt, but make the selection in the shape of the shoulder anyway, as shown here. Use the Navigator palette to zoom in on the image if that helps you make a more accurate selection.

boy_04.jpg

STEP 17. Copying the T-Shirt

Press Ctrl/Command+C to copy the selected T-shirt, and then press Ctrl/Command+V to paste the T-shirt into a new layer named Layer 1 in the image file. Drag the Background layer onto the Delete layer button on the Layers palette to delete the Background layer. Ctrl/Command-click the Layer 1 layer in the Layers palette to reselect the T-shirt.

STEP 18. Correcting the T-Shirt

Choose the Smudge tool from the toolbox, and use it to remove the boy's face in the left shoulder. Drag from the orange material onto the face to smudge the orange color over the face.

STEP 19. Selecting the Harp Image's Background

Choose File, Open (Ctrl/Command+O) and open the Book\Sources\harp.jpg file from the supplementary CD-ROM. Choose the Magic Wand tool from the toolbar, set the Tolerance to 10 on the Options bar, and then click the white area surrounding the harp. Press and hold the Shift key, and then click each of the white areas within the harp and between its strings.

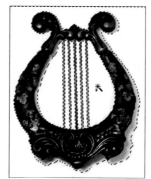

STEP 20. Selecting the Shadow in Quick Mask Mode

Click the Edit in Quick Mask Mode button on the toolbox. The white selection stays white, but the harp image becomes red, indicating that it's masked off. Set the foreground color to white,

choose the Brush tool from the toolbox, and use the Brush Preset picker from the Options bar to choose an appropriate brush. Then, drag along the edges of the mask where needed to remove the harp's shadow from the masked area.

STEP 21. Exiting from the Quick Mask Mode and Copying Only the Harp Image

Click on the Edit in Standard Mode button on the toolbar to return the image, with the mask specifying

areas excluded from the selection frame. Choose Select, Inverse (Shift+Ctrl/Command+I) from the menu bar to invert the selection, so that the image of the harp is now selected. Press Ctrl/Command+C to copy the harp, and then press Ctrl/Command+V to paste the harp selection into a new image layer named Layer 1. Drag the Background layer onto the Delete layer button on the Layers palette to delete the Background layer.

STEP 22. Making a New Blue Image

With the five source images still open in Photoshop, choose File, New (Ctrl/Command+N)

from the menu bar to open the New dialog box. Set the Width to 1200 pixels, the Height to 800 pixels, and the Resolution to 100 pixels/inch. Click the White option under Contents, and then click OK to create a new image file where you'll build the collage. Use the Color palette to set the foreground color to a fairly dark blue, and then use the Paint Bucket tool or press Alt/Option+Del to fill the Background layer with blue.

STEP 23. Importing and Arranging Each Source Object

Use the Move tool from the toolbox to drag each of the five source objects (the boy's head, the hands, the T-shirt, and the harp) to the new image

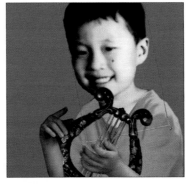

window. A layer for each copied source object appears in the Layers palette. Drag the layers into the following order based on the object each holds, starting from

bottom to top: boy's head, T-shirt, harp, right hand, and left hand. Select each layer in turn; choose Edit, Free Transform (Ctrl/Command+T); adjust the layer object's size, angle, and position as shown here; and then press Enter/Return.

STEP 24. Renaming the Layers

Change the name of each layer as shown here. (To change a layer's name, double-click the name, type a new name, and then press Enter/Return.) As the work becomes more complex, the number of layers will increase dramatically. Both hands in the image have a strong, undesirable blue tone. Click the L-hand layer in the Layers palette to select that layer. Then click the eye icon beside the Harp, T-shirt, and Head layers to hide them.

STEP 25. Correcting the Color of Both Hands

With the L-hand layer still selected in the Layers palette, choose Image, Adjustments, Variations from the menu bar. Click the Original thumbnail to remove previous settings, click the More Red and More Yellow thumbnails once each to make the hand color more natural, and then click OK. Click the R-hand layer in the Layers palette, and then choose Image, Adjustments, Variations from the menu bar. Click the Original thumbnail to remove previous settings, click the More Red and More Yellow thumbnails once each to make the hand color more natural, and then click OK.

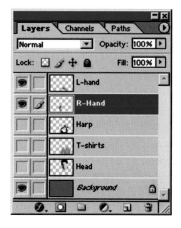

STEP 26. Matching the Color of the Hands

The right hand still appears too yellow. With the R-hand layer still selected in the Layers palette, choose Image, Adjustments, Hue/Saturation (Ctrl/Command+U) from the menu bar to open the Hue/Saturation dialog box. Drag the sliders to specify the settings shown here, and then click OK to make the color match the left hand's.

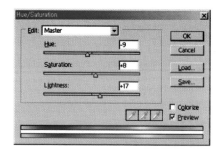

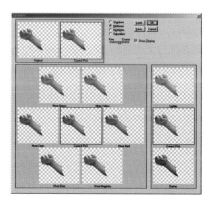

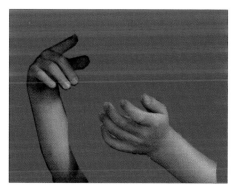

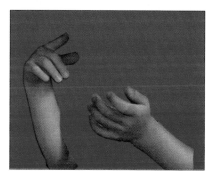

STEP 27.
Making the T-Shirt Black and White

Click the eye icon beside both the L-hand and R-hand layers to hide those layers. Click the T-shirt layer in the Layers palette to both redisplay and select the layer. Choose Image, Adjustments, Desaturate from the menu bar to convert the T-shirt layer contents to black and white.

STEP 28. Lightening the T-Shirt

With the T-shirt layer still selected in the Layers palette, choose Image, Adjustments, Curves (Ctrl/Command+M) from the menu bar. In the Curves dialog box, bend the curve into the shape shown here. To do so, click the diagonal line to create points on the curve, and then drag them into position. Click OK to apply the changes and lighten the T-shirt.

STEP 29. Applying a Blue Tone to the T-Shirt

With the T-shirt layer still selected in the Layers palette, choose Image, Adjustments, Hue/Saturation (Ctrl/Command+U) from the menu bar. In the Hue/Saturation dialog box, click the Colorize check box to check it. Drag the sliders to choose the settings shown here, and then click OK to give the dark areas of the shirt a blue tone.

122   Photoshop 7 Image Effects

STEP 30. Adjusting the Harp's Color

Click the eye icon beside the T-shirt layer to hide the layer. Click the Harp

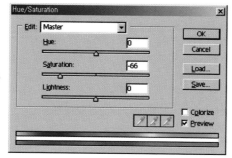

layer in the Layers palette to both redisplay and select the layer. Choose Image, Adjustments,

Hue/Saturation (Ctrl/Command+U) from the menu bar. In the Hue/Saturation dialog box, drag the sliders to choose the settings shown here, and then click OK to convert the harp image to black and white.

STEP 31. Tinting the Harp Brown

With the Harp layer still selected in the Layers palette, choose Image, Adjustments, Hue/Saturation (Ctrl/Command+U) from the menu bar. In the Hue/Saturation dialog box, click the Colorize check box to check it, drag the sliders to choose the settings shown here, and then click OK to tint the harp image brown.

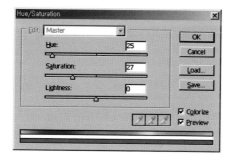

STEP 32. Filling in the Space in the Neck

Click the eye icon beside the Harp layer in the Layers palette to hide that layer, and then click the eye icon box beside both the T-shirt and Head layers to redisplay them. An unwanted space appears between the boy's neck and the V of the shirt. Click the Head layer in the Layers palette to select that layer. Choose the Smudge tool from the toolbox, and then drag down from the neck into the space to smudge the neck area and fill in the empty space. (Zoom in and use the Brush Preset picker on the Options bar to choose an alternative brush size, if those techniques help the process.)

STEP 33. Blurring the Edges of the T-Shirt

The edges of the shirt appear too sharp. Click the T-shirt layer in the Layers palette to select that layer. Choose the Eraser Tool from the toolbox, and then click the Click to open the Brush Preset picker button on the Options bar. Double-click on a softer brush such as the Soft Round 21 pixels brush. Drag along the sharp edges of the shirt to partially erase them.

STEP 34. Adjusting the Harp's Layer Position

Click on the eye icon box beside each hidden layer in the Layers palette to redisplay all the layers. Drag the Harp layer in between the L-hand and R-hand layers. A hidden portion of the harp appears at the bottom, but the harp also hides part of the fingers on the right hand.

STEP 35. Making a Selection in the Shape of the Right Hand

Click the Harp layer in the Layers palette to select that layer. Ctrl/Command-click the R-hand layer to make a selection in the shape of the right hand.

STEP 36. Removing the Area of the Harp that Hides the Fingers

Choose the Eraser tool from the toolbox, and use it to erase the portion of the harp that hides the fingers, using the selection marquee as a guide. (Again, zoom in or change brush sizes if you find it helpful.) Choose Select, Deselect (Ctrl/Command+D) to remove the selection marquee.

STEP 37. Applying a Shadow to the Harp Layer

With the Harp layer still selected in the Layers palette, click the Add a layer style button on the Layers palette, and then click Drop Shadow. Choose the settings shown here in the Layer Style dialog box, and then click OK to apply a shadow to the harp image.

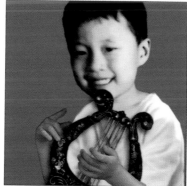

STEP 38. Blurring the Harp Image

The harp appears a bit too sharp compared with the other objects in the image. With the Harp layer still selected in the Layers palette, choose Filter, Blur, Gaussian Blur from the menu. Set the Radius to 1.1 in the Gaussian Blur dialog box, and then click OK to blur the harp image.

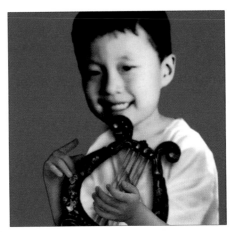

STEP 39. Copying the Shadow to another Layer

In the Layers palette, drag the Drop Shadow choice from the Effects list for the Harp layer below both the L-hand and T-shirt layers to copy the drop shadow to each of the layers.

STEP 40. Softening the Edges of Both Hands

Click the L-hand layer in the Layers palette to select the layer, and then Ctrl/Command-click the L-hand layer to make a selection in the shape of the hand. Choose Select, Inverse (Shift+Ctrl/Command I) from the menu bar to invert the selection. Choose Select, Feather, set the Feature Radius to 2 in the Feather Selection dialog box, and then click OK to soften the edges of the selection frame. Press the Del key two or three times, deleting the area outside the softened selection. Repeat the whole process for the R-hand layer, and then choose Select, Deselect (Ctrl/Command+D) to remove the selection marquee. The hands appear much softer than they did before.

STEP 41. Rotating the Boy

Click the Head layer in the Layers palette to select that layer. Then click the empty box beside each of the layers above the Head layer so that a chain link icon appears, indicating all the layers except the Background layer are now linked. Choose Edit, Free Transform (Ctrl/Command+T) from the menu bar; adjust the boy's size, position, and rotation as shown here; and then press Enter/Return.

STEP 42. Selecting the Wing

Choose File, Open (Ctrl/Command+O) and open the Book\Sources\wing.jpg file from the supplementary CD-ROM. Choose the Polygonal Lasso tool from the toolbox, and then use it to select only the angel's wing.

STEP 43. Adding the Wing to the Project

Choose the Move tool from the toolbox, and then drag the selected wing from the wing.jpg image window onto the window for the project file. The wing appears on its own new layer named Layer 1. Double-click the layer name, type Wing, and press Enter/Return to rename the layer. Drag the Wing layer above the Background layer in the Layers palette. Choose Edit, Free Transform (Ctrl/Command+T) from the menu bar, adjust the size and position of the wing as shown here, and press Enter/Return to finish the transformation.

STEP 44. Making the Other Wing

Copy the Wing layer by dragging it onto the Create a new layer button on the Layers palette. With the new

Wing copy layer selected in the Layers palette, choose Edit, Transform, Flip Horizontal from the menu bar to flip the image of the wing to the other side. Choose the Move tool from the toolbox, and then drag the second wing into position.

STEP 45. Viewing the Completed Angel

Various source images have been added to the picture of the boy to create a cute angel image.

STEP 46. Opening the Flower Image

Choose File, Open (Ctrl/Command+O) and open the Book\Sources\flower.jpg file from the supplementary CD-ROM.

STEP 47. Starting to Extract the Flower

Choose Filter, Extract from the menu bar to open the Extract dialog box. Click the Edge Highlighter tool in the toolbox at the left side of the dialog box. Drag around the flower's outline. Click the Fill tool on the toolbox at the left side of the dialog box, and then click inside of the selected area to designate the area to extract.

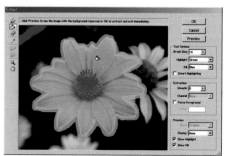

STEP 48. Extracting the Flower

Click the Preview button in the Extract dialog box to see a preview of the area to be extracted. Use the Cleanup and the Edge Touchup tools from the toolbox to refine the edges of the selection, and then click OK to extract the flower.

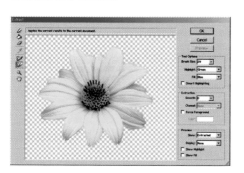

STEP 49. Copying and Sizing the Flower

Choose the Move tool from the toolbox, and then drag the extracted flower from the flower.jpg image window onto the project image window, where it appears on its own new layer named Layer 1. With Layer 1 selected in the Layers palette, choose Edit, Free Transform (Ctrl/Command+T) from the menu bar. Adjust the size and position of the flower, as shown here, and then press Enter/Return to finish the transformation.

STEP 50. Saving the Flower as a Brush

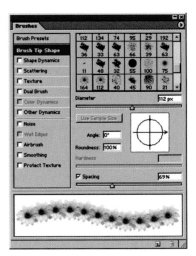

In the Layers palette, double-click on the Layer 1 layer name, type "flower," and then press Enter/Return to rename the layer. Ctrl/Command-click on the flower layer to make a selection in the shape of the flower. Choose Edit, Define Brush from the menu bar. Type a name for the brush in the Name text box of the Brush Name dialog box, and click OK to save the flower as a brush. Choose the Brush tool from the toolbox. Click the Click to open the Brush Preset picker button on the Options bar. Scroll down through the available brushes, and then double-click the newly created brush at the bottom of the list. Click the Toggle the Brushes palette button on the Options bar to open the Brushes palette. Click Brush Tip Shape in the list on the left, and then change the Spacing setting to 69% to increase the spacing between the flowers.

STEP 51. Adjusting the Brush

Click the Shape Dynamics check box in the list at the left side of the Brushes palette, and then increase the Size Jitter and Angle Jitter settings to randomize the size and rotation of the brush. Click the Scattering check box in the list at the left, and then increase the Scatter value to scatter the flowers created with the brush. Click the palette's close button to close the palette window.

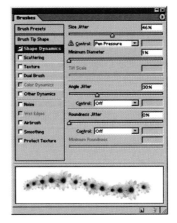
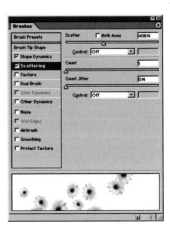

STEP 52. Adding Flowers with the Flower Brush

With the flower layer still selected in the Layers palette, choose Select, Deselect (Ctrl/Command+D) to remove the selection marquee. Click the Default Foreground and Background Colors button on the toolbox to reset the foreground color to black and the background color to white. Press Ctrl/Command+Del to fill the layer with white. Choose the Brush tool from the toolbox, and drag it across the layer to create scattered flowers over the layer. Drag the flower layer below the Wing layer in the Layers palette.

STEP 53. Removing the White Background from the Flower Layer

Choose the Magic Wand tool from the toolbox, and then click on the white background on the flower layer. Press Del to delete the white background from the layer, and then choose Select, Deselect (Ctrl/Command+D) to remove the selection marquee.

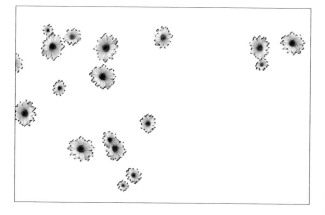

STEP 54. Tinting the Flower Layer Red

With the flower layer still selected in the Layers palette, choose Image, Adjustments, Hue/Saturation (Ctrl/Command+U) from the menu bar. Click the Colorize check box in the Hue/Saturation dialog box to check it, drag the sliders to choose the settings shown here, and then click OK to tint the flowers red.

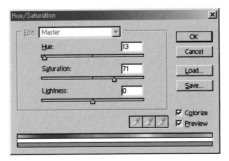

STEP 55. Adding Yellow to the Flower Layer

With the flower layer still selected in the Layers palette, choose Image, Adjustments, Variations from the menu bar. Click the More Yellow thumbnail in the Variations dialog box several times, and then click OK to add a yellowish tone to the flowers.

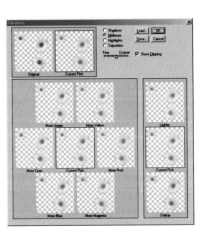

STEP 56. Applying Shadows to the Flower Layer

With the flower layer still selected in the Layers palette, click the Add a layer style button, and then click Drop Shadow. Click OK in the Layer Style dialog box to add a shadow as shown here. Click the Background layer in the Layers palette to select the layer, and then choose Filter, Render, Lighting Effects from the menu bar. Drag the handles in the Preview area to change the direction and spread of the light source as shown here, and then click OK to add the lighting effects to the Background layer.

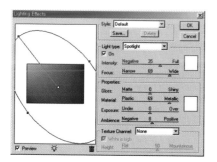

STEP 57. Adding Text to Complete the Image

Choose the Horizontal Type tool from the toolbox, display the Character palette to adjust text settings and to add the text that appears to be buried in the background. With the new text layer selected in the Layers palette, open the Layer Style drop-down list from the upper-left corner of the Layers palette, and then click Soft Light. Also use the Opacity slider on the Layers palette to change the layer's Opacity setting to 47%. Click the Background layer in the Layers palette, and then click the Create a new layer button (Shift+Ctrl/Command+N) to add a new layer named Layer 1. Choose Filter, Render, Clouds to fill Layer 1 with a cloud texture. With Layer 1 selected in the Layers palette, open the Layer Style drop-down list from the upper-left corner of the Layers palette, and then click Soft Light. Also use the Opacity slider on the Layers palette to change the layer's opacity setting to 47%.

STEP 58. Rearranging to a Wide Layout

Use the Image, Image Size command to increase the width of the image file as desired. Then drag items on their layers as desired. If you like, blend a horizontal stripe pattern using the Overlay blend mode to emphasize the expansion of the image across the horizontal.

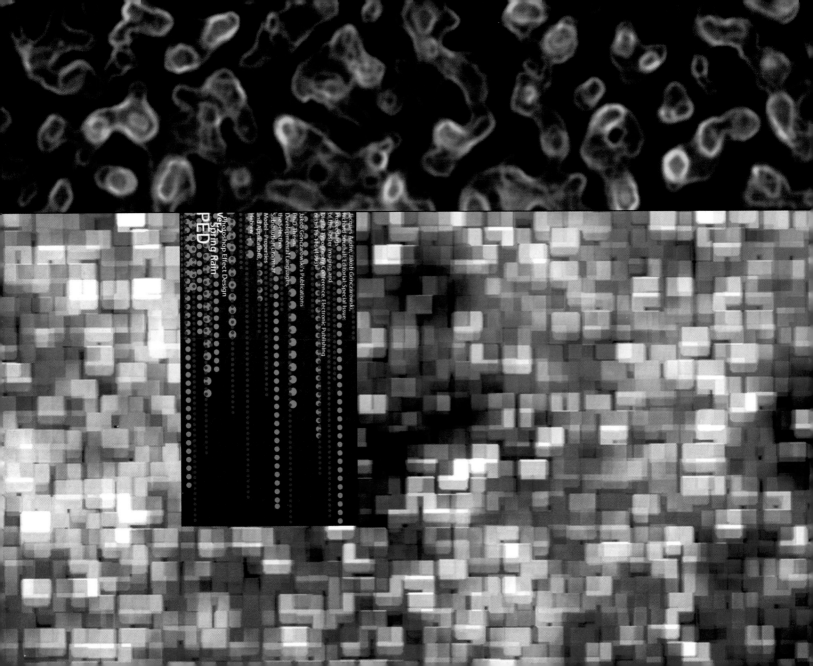

Project 11: Spring Rain

You can use Photoshop's powerful brush features to draw dotted lines. Using a round brush shape to make dots with a variety of sizes, create an image of falling raindrops.

Spring Rain

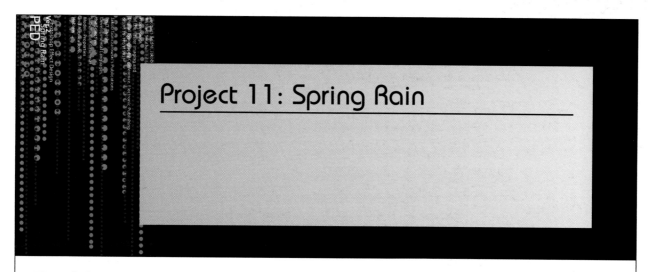

Project 11: Spring Rain

Total Steps

STEP 1. Making a New Image with a Black Background

STEP 2. Making a Dotted Brush

STEP 3. Drawing Dotted Lines

STEP 4. Adjusting the Brush Size

STEP 5. Overlapping Varying Sizes of Dotted Images

STEP 6. Adding the Title

STEP 7. Adding Vertical Text to Complete the Image

STEP 1. Making a New Image with a Black Background

Choose File, New (Ctrl/Command+N) from the menu bar to open the New dialog box. Set the Width to 400 pixels and the Height to 700 pixels. Set the Resolution to 150 pixels/inch, make sure that White is selected under Contents, and then click OK to create a new image. Set the foreground color to a dark gray, and then use the Paint Bucket tool or press Alt/Option+Del to fill the Background layer with dark gray.

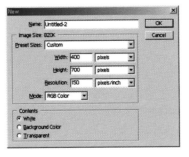

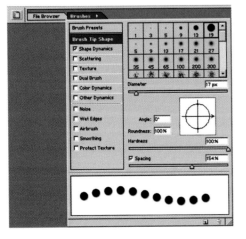

STEP 2. Making a Dotted Brush

Choose the Brush tool from the toolbox, and then click the Toggle the Brushes Palette button on the Options bar to open the Brushes palette. Click Brush Tip Shape in the list at the left, and then click the Hard Round 19 pixels brush at the right. Drag the Diameter and Spacing sliders to set the values shown here. Increasing the Spacing value makes the brush stroke look like a series of dots. Click the Close button on the Brushes palette to close the palette.

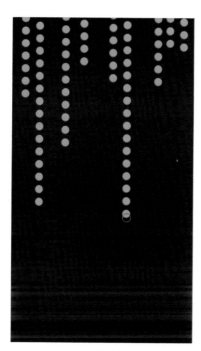

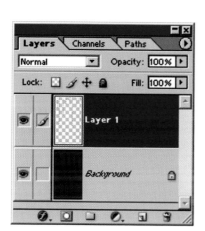

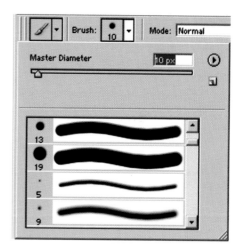

STEP 3. Drawing Dotted Lines

Click the Create a new layer button (Shift+Ctrl/Command+N) in the Layers palette to add a new layer named Layer 1. Use the Color palette to set the foreground color to an aqua color, and then draw some vertical lines from the top of the image, as shown here. Press and hold the Shift key after you start dragging to ensure a straight line.

STEP 4. Adjusting the Brush Size

Click the Click to open the Brush Preset picker button on the Options bar, drag the Master Diameter slider to adjust the brush size as shown here, and then click the Click to open the Brush Preset picker button again to close the preset picker. (You also could use the Brushes palette to adjust the Brush size, if you prefer.)

STEP 5. Overlapping Varying Sizes of Dotted Images

Click the Create a new layer button (Shift+Ctrl/Command+N) in the Layers palette to add a new layer named Layer 1. Use the Color palette to set the foreground color to a chartreuse color, and then draw additional vertical lines. Repeat Steps 5 and 6, changing the brush size and foreground color and then drawing vertical lines, until you are satisfied with the result.

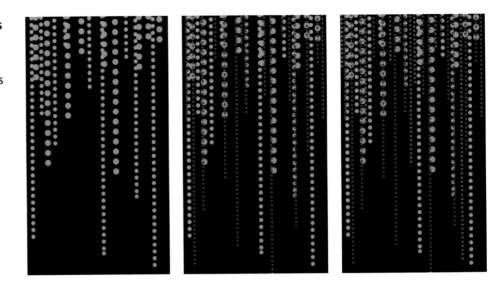

STEP 6. Adding the Title

Choose the Horizontal Type tool from the toolbox, and then display the Character palette and use it to choose the desired font and size, as well as a white text color. Click in the image window, type the title as shown here, and then click the Commit any current edits button on the Options bar. The text appears on a new layer in the Layers palette.

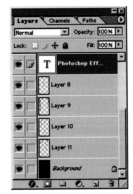

STEP 7. Adding Vertical Text to Complete the Image

With the text layer still selected in the Layers palette, choose Edit, Transform, Rotate from the menu bar. Drag a handle to rotate the text clockwise 90°. Press and hold the Shift key while rotating the text to rotate with precision, and then press Enter/Return to finish the transformation. Use the Horizontal Type tool to enter the remaining text shown here, and then rotate it as well to complete the image.

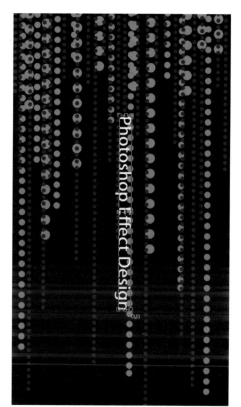

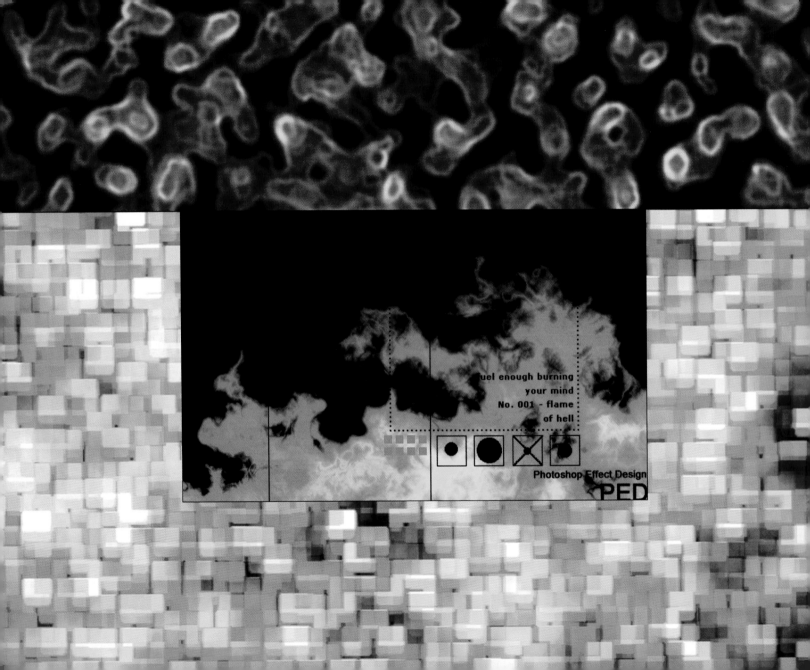

fuel enough burning
your mind
No. 001 - flame
of hell

Photoshop Effect Design
PED

Project 12: Realistic Flame

In this project, create a burning flame. See how to use the Clouds and Difference Clouds filters to create this texture.

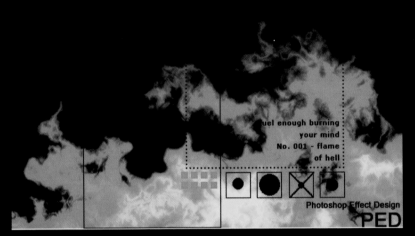

Realistic Flame

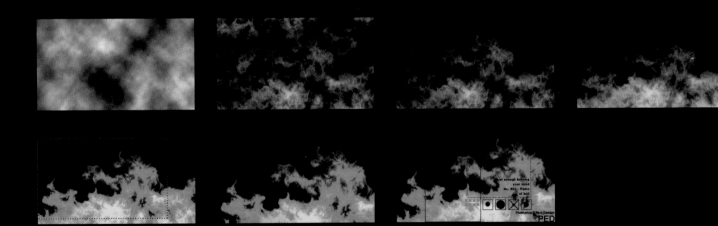

Project 12: Realistic Flame

Photoshop Effect Design
PED

Total Steps

STEP 1. Making a New Image

STEP 2. Adding a Cloud Texture

STEP 3. Making the Cloud Texture More Complex

STEP 4. Defining the Flame Shapes

STEP 5. Removing Unwanted Areas

STEP 6. Adding a Gradient Layer

STEP 7. Blending the Gradient Layer

STEP 8. Coloring the Flames

STEP 9. Completing the Flame Image

STEP 1. Making a New Image

Choose File, New (Ctrl/Command+N) from the menu bar to open the New dialog box. Set the Width to 800 pixels and the Height to 450 pixels. Set the Resolution to 150 pixels/inch, make sure that White is selected under Contents, and then click OK to create a new image.

STEP 2. Adding a Cloud Texture

Click the Default Foreground and Background Colors button in the toolbox to make the foreground color black and the background color white. Then, choose Filter, Render, Clouds from the menu bar to fill the Background layer with a cloud texture. Press Ctrl/Command+F to reapply the filter until the clouds reach the desired appearance.

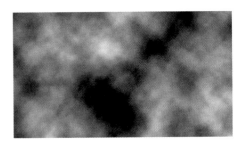

STEP 3. Making the Cloud Texture More Complex

Choose Filter, Render, Difference Clouds from the menu bar. The Difference Clouds filter effect blends with the Clouds filter effect, creating a more complex shape. Continue to press Ctrl/Command+F (at least three to five times) until you see flame shapes along the bottom of the image.

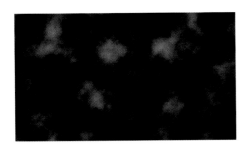
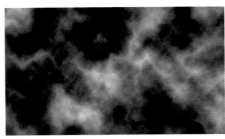

STEP 4. Defining the Flame Shapes

With the foreground color still set to black, choose the Brush tool from the toolbox. Click the Click to open the Brush Preset picker button on the Options bar, drag the Master Diameter slider to set the brush size to 10, and then click the Click to open the Brush Preset picker button again to close the preset picker. (If needed, also display the Brushes palette, click Brush Tip Shape at the left, and then drag the Spacing slider so you get a solid line rather than the dot pattern from the previous project.) Identify the areas of flame shape that you want to keep, and use the Brush to color around them in black, more clearly defining the flame shape.

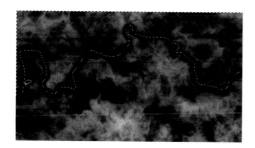

STEP 5. Removing Unwanted Areas

Choose the Lasso tool from the toolbox, and use it to select the areas of texture above the flame shape that you want to retain in the image. With the foreground color still set to black, use the Paint Bucket tool or press Alt/Option+Del to fill the selection with black. Choose Select, Deselect (Ctrl/Command+D) to remove the selection marquee.

STEP 6. Adding a Gradient Layer

Click the Create a new layer button (Shift+Ctrl/Command+N) in the Layers palette to add a new layer named Layer 1. With the default foreground and background colors still selected, choose the Gradient tool from the toolbox. Click the Linear Gradient button on the Options bar, and then drag from the top to the bottom of the image window to apply a gradient to the new layer, as shown here.

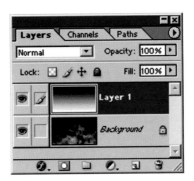

STEP 7. Blending the Gradient Layer

With Layer 1 still selected in the Layers palette, open the Layer Style drop-down list in the upper-left corner of the Layers palette, and then click Soft Light to make the lower portion of the image brighter. Click the palette menu button in the upper-right corner of the Layers palette, and then click Merge Down to merge the layers.

STEP 8. Coloring the Flames

Now change the gradient colors to black, red, and yellow to make the flames look realistic. Choose Image, Adjustments, Gradient Map from the menu bar. Click the gradient in the Gradient Used for Grayscale Mapping box of the Gradient Map dialog box to open the Gradient Editor dialog box. Click the first gradient preset in the Presets area, and then create two more color stops at the bottom of the gradient preview to include additional gradient colors. To set up a stop, click the bottom of the gradient preview, and then use the Color box at the bottom of the dialog box to choose the color for that stop. Double-click on the far right color stop to change its color, and then drag it left to move it to the position shown here. (You can delete a color stop by dragging it down off the bottom of the preview.) Click OK to close the Gradient Editor dialog box, and then click OK again to apply the gradient.

STEP 9. Completing the Flame Image

Choose the Rectangular Marquee tool from the toolbox, and drag to select the portion of the image that you want to include in your final composition. Choose Image, Crop from the menu bar to delete areas outside the selection. You can then add text and other elements to the image as desired.

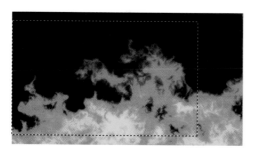

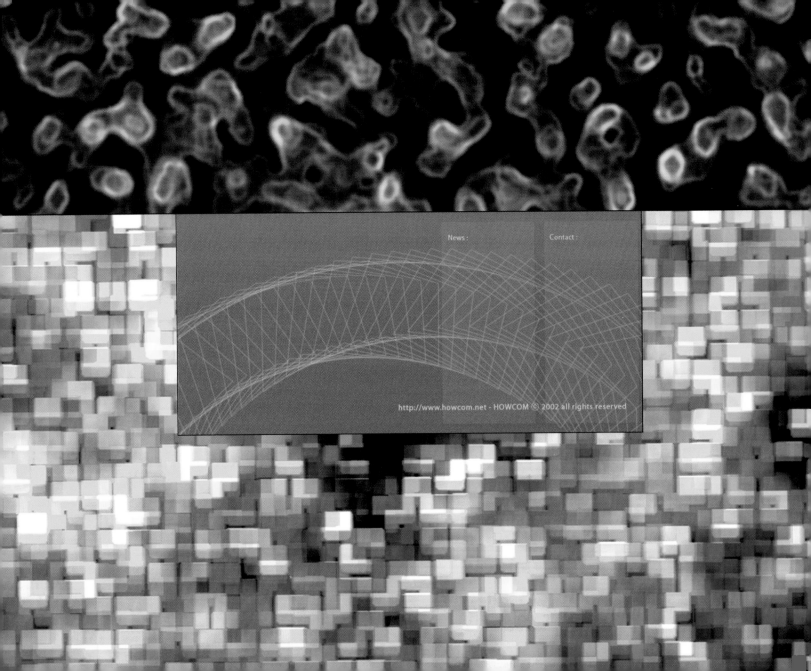

Project 13: Wire Frame Bridge

You can use Photoshop's Brush tool to create a wire frame effect that normally requires a 3-D graphics program. In this project, you will create a wire frame bridge.

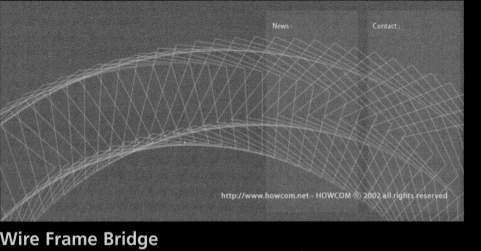

Wire Frame Bridge

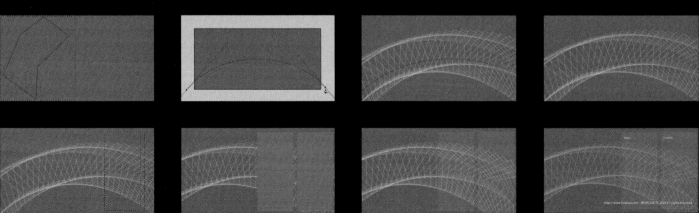

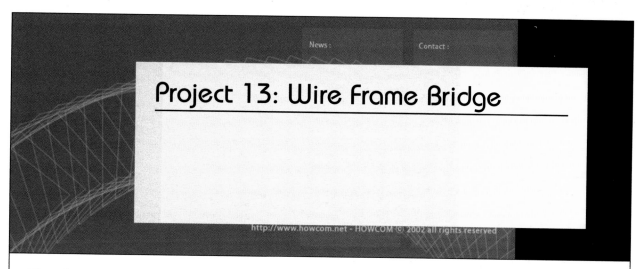

Total Steps

STEP 1. Making a New Image with a Pea Green Background

STEP 2. Creating the Wire Frame Shape on a New Layer

STEP 3. Saving the Wire Frame as a Brush

STEP 4. Selecting the Wire Frame Brush

STEP 5. Adding Rotation to the Brush

STEP 6. Stroking the Path with the Wire Frame Brush

STEP 7. Selecting Two Rectangles

STEP 8. Filling the Rectangles

STEP 9. Adding Text to Complete the Image

STEP 1. Making a New Image with a Pea Green Background

Choose File, New (Ctrl/Command+N) from the menu bar to open the New dialog box. Set the Width to 800 pixels and the Height to 350 pixels. Set the Resolution to 150 pixels/inch, make sure that White is selected under Contents, and click OK to create a new image. Use the Color palette to set the foreground color to a dark pea green (R:136, G:136, B:0), and then use the Paint Bucket tool or press Alt/Option+Del to fill the Background layer with the green color.

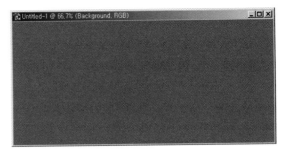

STEP 2. Creating the Wire Frame Shape on a New Layer

Click the Create a new layer button (Shift+Ctrl/Command+N) in the Layers palette to add a new layer named Layer 1. Choose the Paint Brush tool from the toolbox. Click the Click to open the Brush Preset picker button on the Options bar, drag the Master Diameter slider to set the brush size to 1, and then click the Click to open the Brush Preset picker button again to close the preset picker. Click the Default Foreground and Background Colors button on the toolbox to reset the foreground color to black, and then use the Navigator palette to zoom in. Draw the shape shown here by clicking the first point, and then pressing and holding the Shift key and clicking additional points— the corners of the shape. (Note that you can hide the Background layer temporarily to make it easier to see the shape that you're drawing.)

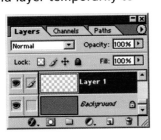

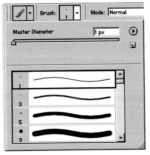

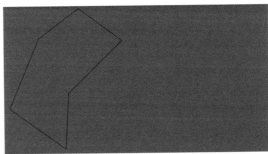

STEP 3. Saving the Wire Frame as a Brush

With the Layer 1 layer still selected in the Layers palette, choose Select, Load Selection from the menu bar. Make sure Layer 1 Transparency is selected from the Channel drop-down list, and then click OK to select the wire frame shape on the layer. Choose Edit, Define Brush from the menu bar to open the Brush Name dialog box. Type a new Name for the brush if desired, and then click OK to save the shape as a brush. Choose Select, Deselect (Ctrl/Command+D) to remove the selection marquee.

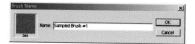

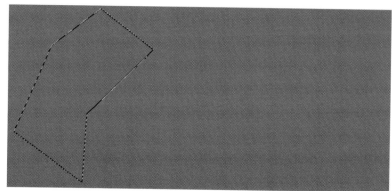

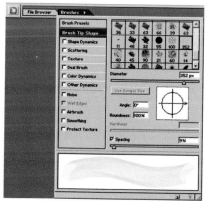

STEP 4. Selecting the Wire Frame Brush

Choose the Brush tool from the toolbox, and click the Toggle the Brushes palette button on the Options bar. Click Brush Presets at the top of the list at the left, scroll down the list of brushes at the right, and click the new brush at the bottom of the list. Click Brush Tip Shape in the list at the left, and then set the Spacing to 9% as shown here.

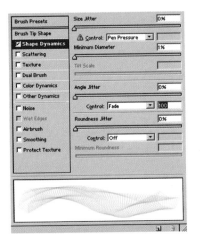

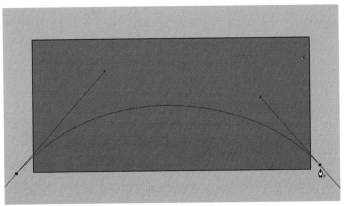

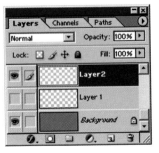

STEP 5. Adding Rotation to the Brush

Click Shape Dynamics in the list at the left side of the Brushes palette. Open the Control drop-down list under Angle Jitter, and then click Fade in the drop-down list. This selects the value in the text box to the right of the Control drop-down list. Type "100" to replace the existing value. This setting will cause the brush angle to rotate slowly, making one revolution per 100 repetitions of the shape when you drag the brush. Click the Close button on the Brushes palette to close the palette.

Click the eye icon beside Layer 1 in the Layers palette to hide that layer. Click the Create a new layer button (Shift+Ctrl/Command+N) on the Layers palette to add a new layer named Layer 2. Choose the Pen tool from the toolbox, and then click the Paths button on the Options bar to specify that you want to draw a work path. Then, use the Pen tool to draw the path shown here. Then, use the Direct Selection tool from the toolbox to drag on the handles on either end of the path to adjust the shape of the path. Press Enter/Return to finish editing the path.

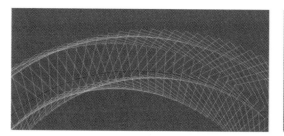 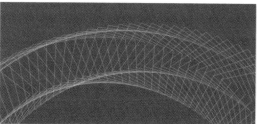 

STEP 6. Stroking the Path with the Wire Frame Brush

Choose Window, Paths from the menu bar to open the Paths palette. The path you just drew appears as a path named Work Path. Set the foreground color to white, and choose the Brush tool from the toolbox. The Brush box on the Options bar shows that the wire frame brush you made earlier is still selected as the current brush. Click the Work Path choice in the Paths layer, and then click the Stroke path with brush button at the bottom of the palette. A wire frame bridge appears along the path. Click the gray area below the path in the Paths palette to hide the path. Choose Window, Layers to redisplay the Layers palette.

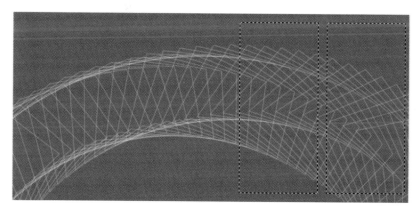

STEP 7. Selecting Two Rectangles

Click the Create a new layer button (Shift+Ctrl/Command+N) on the Layers palette to add a new layer named Layer 3. Choose the Rectangular Marquee tool from the toolbox, and drag to select two rectangles at the right side of the image, as shown here. Press and hold the Shift key after you draw the first rectangle to add the second rectangle.

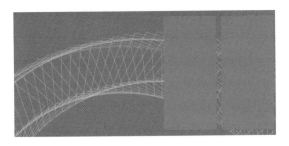 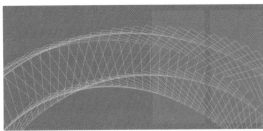 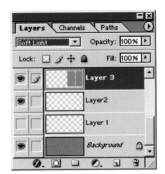

STEP 8. Filling the Rectangles

Use the Colors palette to set the foreground color to a yellow green, and then use the Paint Bucket tool or press Alt/Option+Del to fill the selection with yellow green. With Layer 3 still selected in the Layers palette, open the Layer Style drop-down list in the upper-left corner of the Layers palette, and then click Soft Light to blend the blocks of color. Choose Select, Deselect (Ctrl/Command+D) from the menu bar to remove the selection marquee.

STEP 9. Adding Text to Complete the Image

Use the Horizontal Type tool and Character palette to add text in a bright yellow green color as shown here to complete this image. You could use an image like this as a sub-page for a Web site.

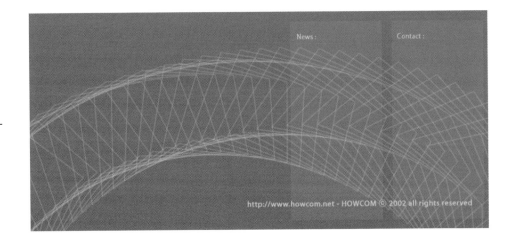

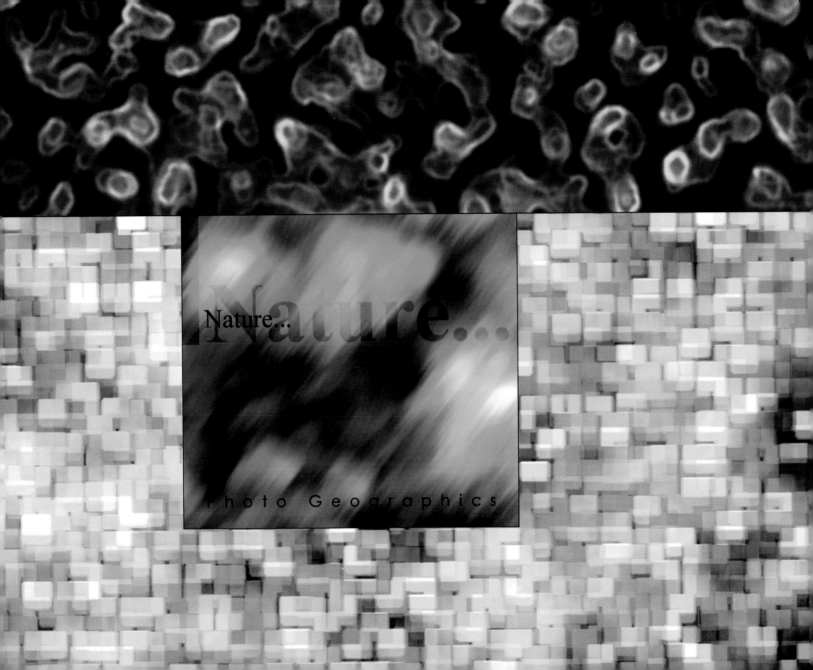

Nature...

Photo Geographics

Project 14: Forest Light

In this project, learn to portray the rays of sunlight that peek through the leaves in a dense forest. Although the end result will not be as sharp and focused as a photograph, use Photoshop filters to create a unique and mysterious image.

Nature..

Nature...

Nature..

Photo Geographics

Project 14: Forest Light

Nature...

Photo Geographics

Total Steps

STEP 1. Making a New Image

STEP 2. Adding a Cloud Texture

STEP 3. Applying the Palette Knife Filter to the Cloud Texture

STEP 4. Adding Green and Yellow Tones to the Texture

STEP 5. Rotating the Image

STEP 6. Adding Wind

STEP 7. Blurring the Windblown Effect

STEP 8. Blurring the Image Again

STEP 9. Cropping the Rotated Rectangle

STEP 10. Cropping to Create a Smaller Image

STEP 11. Adding, Copying, and Sizing the Title

STEP 12. Blending the Title to Complete the Image

STEP 1. Making a New Image

Choose File, New (Ctrl/Command+N) from the menu bar to open the New dialog box. Set the Width to 600 pixels and the Height to 800 pixels. Set the Resolution to 150 pixels/inch, make sure that White is selected under Contents, and then click OK to create a new image.

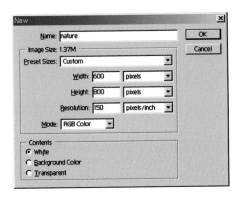

STEP 2. Adding a Cloud Texture

Click the Default Foreground and Background Colors button on the toolbar to make the foreground color black and the background color white. Choose Filter, Render, Difference Clouds from the menu bar to fill the Background layer with a cloud texture. Press Ctrl+F at least five times to reapply the filter and create the complex texture seen here.

STEP 3. Applying the Palette Knife Filter to the Cloud Texture

Choose Filter, Artistic, Palette Knife from the menu bar to open the Palette Knife dialog box. Choose the settings shown here, and then click OK to give the cloud texture a mottled appearance.

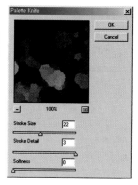

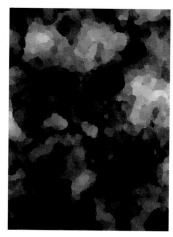

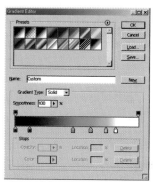

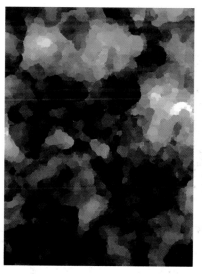

STEP 4. Adding Green and Yellow Tones to the Texture

Choose Image, Adjustments, Gradient Map from the menu bar to open the Gradient Map dialog box. Click the gradient in the Gradient Used for Grayscale Mapping box of the Gradient Map dialog box to open the Gradient Editor dialog box. Click the first gradient preset in the Presets area, and then create four more color stops at the bottom of the gradient preview to include additional gradient colors. To set up a stop, click the bottom of the gradient preview, and then use the Color box at the bottom of the dialog box to choose the color for that stop. Drag the far right color stop left to move it to the position shown here. (You can delete a color stop by dragging it down off the bottom of the preview.) Click OK to close the Gradient Editor dialog box, and then click OK again to apply the gradient.

STEP 5. Rotating the Image

Choose Image, Rotate Canvas, Arbitrary from the menu bar to open the Rotate Canvas dialog box. Set the Angle to 50, click the CW option button, and then click OK to rotate the image 50° clockwise. The image window increases in size to accommodate the rotated rectangle.

STEP 6. Adding Wind

Choose Filter, Stylize, Wind from the menu bar to open the Wind dialog box. Click Blast under Method, make sure the From the Right option button is selected, and then click OK.

Choose Filter, Stylize, Wind again. This time, click Wind under Method for a softer effect, leave From the Right selected, and then click OK. Press Ctrl/Command+F to apply the Wind filter one last time, emphasizing the windblown effect.

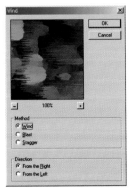
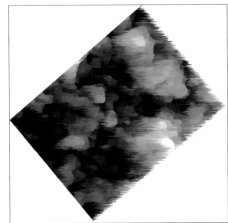

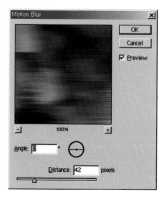
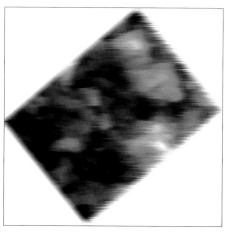

STEP 7. Blurring the Windblown Effect

Choose Filter, Blur, Motion Blur from the menu bar to open the Motion Blur dialog box. Choose the settings shown here, and then click OK to blur the image horizontally, adding the appearance of motion and velocity to the image.

STEP 8. Blurring the Image Again

Choose Filter, Blur, Gaussian Blur from the menu bar to open the Gaussian Blur dialog box. Set the Radius to 2, and then click OK to blur the image.

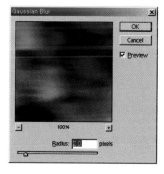
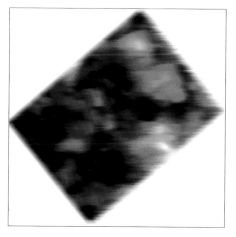

STEP 9. Cropping the Rotated Rectangle

Choose the Crop tool from the toolbox. Drag on
the image to establish a crop area. Drag handles to
rotate and size the crop area to select the rotated
rectangle shape as shown here, and then press
Enter/Return to crop the image. Choose Image,
Rotate Canvas, 90° CCW to rotate the image so that
the angle of the blurring runs up and to the right.

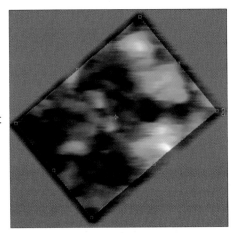

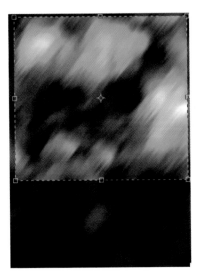

STEP 10. Cropping to Create a Smaller Image

Choose the Crop tool from the
toolbox again. Drag on the image to
specify a smaller size for the image,
and then press Enter/Return to crop
the image.

STEP 11. Adding, Copying, and Sizing the Title

Choose the Horizontal Type tool from the toolbox, click the Toggle the Character and Paragraph palettes button to open the Character palette if needed, and then use the Character palette to choose a font and font size. Click in the

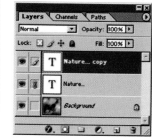

image, type "Nature..." as the title, and then click the Commit any current edits button on the Options bar to finish adding the title. Copy the Nature... layer by dragging it onto the Create a new layer button on the Layers palette. With the new Nature... copy layer selected in the Layers palette, choose Edit, Free Transform (Ctrl/Command+T). Use the handles that appear to increase the text size as shown here, and then press Enter/Return to finish the transformation. Click the empty box beside the Nature... layer so that a chain link appears, linking the layers.

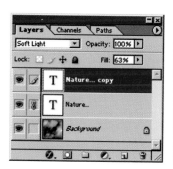

STEP 12. Blending the Title to Complete the Image

With the Nature... copy layer selected in the Layers palette, open the Layer Style drop-down list from the upper-left corner of the Layers palette, and then click Soft Light. Also use the Fill slider on the Layers palette to change the layer's Fill setting to 63%, making the text semi-transparent. Then, use the Horizontal Type tool to add the remaining text, as well as adding a filled and blending rectangle in the upper-left corner of the image.

Movement

The word tempo is used as an image as much as a word through the combination of scale with speed and time.

Project 15: A Cube Mosaic

In this project, fill a layer with cubes and vary their texture and color to create a 3-D mosaic effect. Various blending modes emphasize the mosaic texture.

The word tempo is used as an image as much as a word through the combination of scale with speed and time.

Movement

A Cube Mosaic

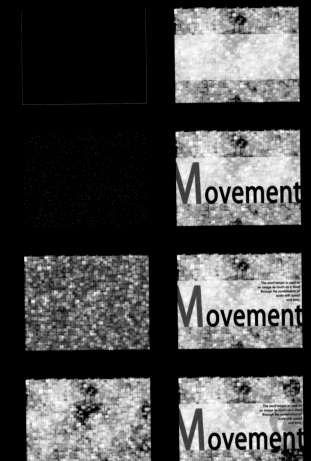

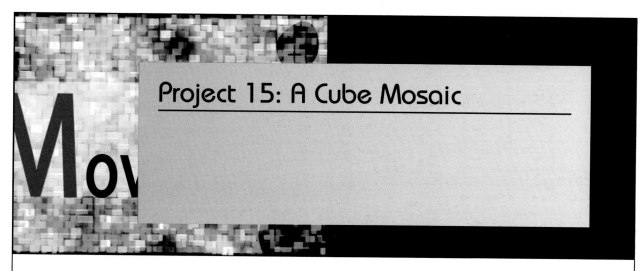

Project 15: A Cube Mosaic

Total Steps

STEP 1. Making a New Image with a Black Background

STEP 2. Adding Black and White Noise

STEP 3. Creating Mosaic Tiles

STEP 4. Adding Dimension to the Tiles

STEP 5. Adding and Blending a Cloud Texture Layer

STEP 6. Adding Color to the Tiles

STEP 7. Adding a Turquoise Layer

STEP 8. Blending the Turquoise Layer

STEP 9. Adding a Semitransparent White Band

STEP 10. Adding and Resizing the Title

STEP 11. Making the First Letter Brown

STEP 12. Adding the Remaining Text

STEP 13. Adding a Human Shape to Complete the Image

STEP 1. Making a New Image with a Black Background

Choose File, New (Ctrl/Command+N) from the menu bar to open the New dialog box. Set the Width to 800 pixels and the Height to 600 pixels. Set the Resolution to 100 pixels/inch, make sure that White is selected under Contents, and click OK to create a new image. Click the Default Foreground and Background Colors button on the toolbox to set the foreground color to black, and then use the Paint Bucket tool or press Alt/Option+Del to fill the Background layer with black.

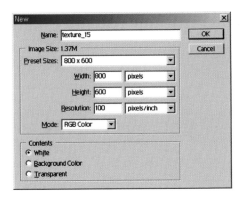

STEP 2. Adding Black and White Noise

Choose Filter, Noise, Add Noise from the menu bar to open the Noise dialog box. Click the Monochromatic check box to check it, set the Amount to 100, and then click OK to apply black and white noise to the Background layer.

STEP 3. Creating Mosaic Tiles

Choose Filter, Texture, Patchwork from the menu bar to open the Patchwork dialog box. Choose the settings shown here, and then click OK to fill the Background layer with uniform mosaic tiles.

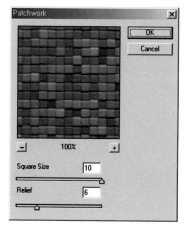

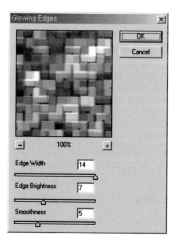

STEP 4. Adding Dimension to the Tiles

Choose Filter, Stylize, Glowing Edges to open the Glowing Edges dialog box. Choose the settings shown here, and then click OK to emphasize some tiles and add dimension to the image.

STEP 5. Adding and Blending a Cloud Texture Layer

Click the Create a new layer button (Shift+Ctrl/Command+N) on the Layers palette to make a new layer named Layer 1. With the foreground color still set to black, use the Paint Bucket tool or press Alt/Option+Del to fill Layer 1

  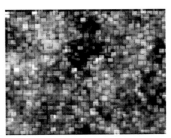

with black. Choose Filter, Render, Difference Clouds from the menu bar to fill Layer 1 with a cloud pattern. If desired, reapply (Ctrl/Command+F) and remove (Ctrl/Command+Z) until the cloud texture achieves the appearance you prefer. With Layer 1 still selected in the Layers palette, open the Layer Style drop-down list from the upper-left corner of the Layers palette, and then click Overlay to apply the mottled tones of the cloud to the mosaic.

STEP 6. Adding Color to the Tiles

Click the Create new fill or adjustment layer button on the Layers palette, and then click Gradient Map in the menu that appears. The Gradient Map dialog box will open. Click the gradient in the Gradient Used for Grayscale Mapping box of the Gradient Map dialog box to open the Gradient Editor dialog box. Click the first gradient preset in the Presets area, and then create three more color stops at the bottom of the gradient preview to include additional gradient colors. To set up a stop, click the bottom of the gradient preview, and then use the Color box at the bottom of the dialog box to choose the color for that stop. Drag the far right color stop left to move it to the position shown here. (You can delete a color stop by dragging it down off the bottom of the preview.) Click OK to close the Gradient Editor dialog box, and then click OK again to apply the gradient.

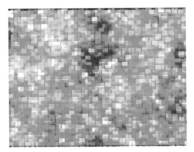

STEP 7. Adding a Turquoise Layer

Click the Create a new layer button (Shift+Ctrl/Command+N) on the Layers palette to add a new layer named Layer 2. Use the Color palette to set the foreground color to a turquoise color (R:3, G:158, B:160), and then use the Paint Bucket tool or press Alt/Option+Del to fill the layer with turquoise.

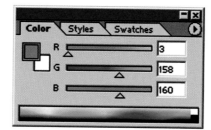

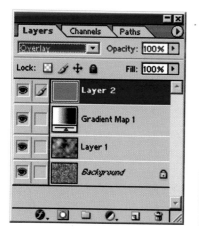

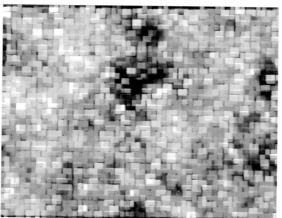

STEP 8. Blending the Turquoise Layer

With Layer 2 still selected in the Layers palette, open the Layer Style drop-down list from the upper-left corner of the Layers palette, and then click Overlay to mix the turquoise color with the mosaic.

STEP 9. Adding a Semitransparent White Band

Click the Create a new layer button (Shift+Ctrl/Command+N) on the Layers palette to add a new layer named Layer 3. Set the foreground color to white. Choose the Rectangular Marquee tool from the toolbox, drag to select a wide

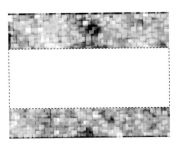

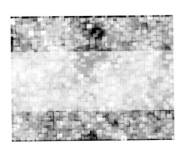

band across the image, and then use the Paint Bucket tool or press Alt/Option+Del to fill the selection with white. Choose Select, Deselect (Ctrl/Command+D) from the menu bar to remove the selection marquee. With Layer 3 still selected, use the Opacity slider on the Layers palette to change the Layer 3 Opacity setting to 70%.

STEP 10. Adding and Resizing the Title

Click the Default Foreground and Background Colors button on the toolbox to set the foreground color to black. Choose the Horizontal Type tool from the toolbox, click the Toggle the Character and Paragraph palettes button to open the Character palette if needed, and then use the Character palette to choose a font and font size. Click in the image, type "Movement" as the title, and then click the Commit any current edits button on the Options bar to finish adding the

title. Choose Edit, Transform, Scale from the menu bar, drag the handles to increase the text size to fill the white band, and then press Enter/Return to finish the transformation.

STEP 11. Making the First Letter Brown

With the Horizontal Type tool still selected, drag over the letter M on the Movement layer. Use the Color palette to specify a dark brown color (R:159, G:16, B:0), and then click the Commit any current edits button on the Options bar to finish applying the brown color to the letter M.

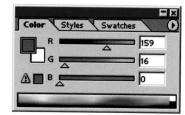

STEP 12. Adding the Remaining Text

Click the Create a new layer button (Shift+Ctrl/Command+N) on the Layers palette to make a new layer named Layer 4. Choose the font settings shown here in the Character palette. Click the Paragraph palette tab, and then click the Right align text button. Then click on the new layer, type the remaining text as shown here, and click the Commit any current edits button on the Options bar.

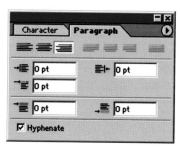

The word tempo is used as an image as much as a word through the combination of scale with speed and time.

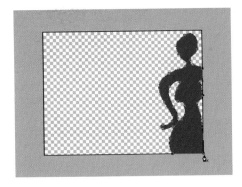

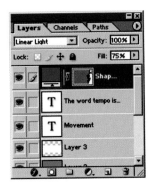

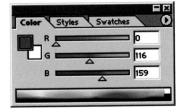

STEP 13. Adding a Human Shape to Complete the Image

Use the Color palette to set the foreground color to a blue green color (R:0, G:116, B:159). Choose the Pen tool from the toolbox, click the Shape layers button on the Options bar to add a new shape layer, and then draw a simple human shape at the right side of the image. With the Shape 1 layer still selected in the Layers palette, open the Layer Style drop-down list from the upper-left corner of the Layers palette, and then click Linear Light. Also use the Fill slider on the Layers palette to change the Fill setting for the layer to 75%, blending the person nicely with the rest of the image. (To hide the path points, choose Window, Paths; click a gray area within the palette; and then choose Window, Layers to redisplay the Layers palette.)

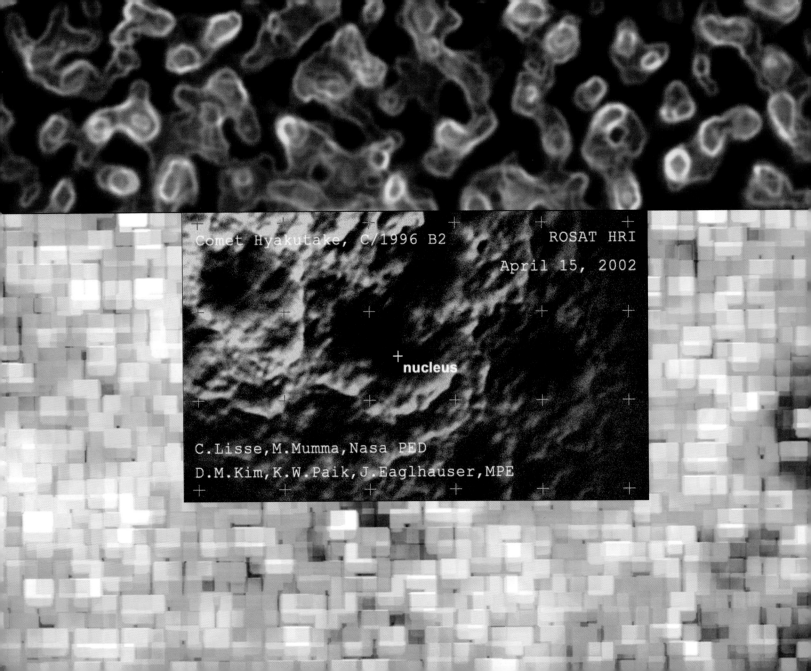

Comet Hyakutake, C/1996 B2   ROSAT HRI

April 15, 2002

+ nucleus

C.Lisse,M.Mumma,Nasa PED

D.M.Kim,K.W.Paik,J.Eaglhauser,MPE

Project 16: Satellite Photography

You can use the Clouds and Lighting Effects filters to make an image that looks like a satellite photograph.

Comet Hyakutake, C/1996 B2   ROSAT HRI
April 15, 2002

+ nucleus

C.Lisse,M.Mumma,Nasa PED
D.M.Kim,K.W.Paik,J.Eaglhauser,MPE

Satellite Photography

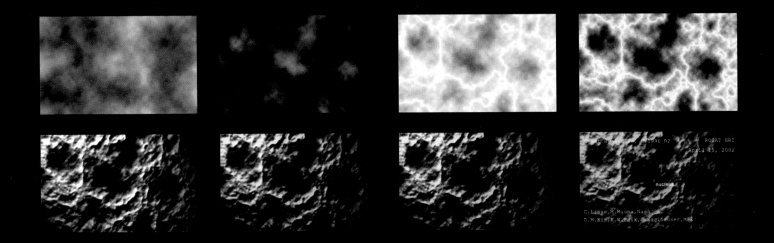

Project 16: Satellite Photography

Comet Hyakutake, C/1996 B2   ROSAT HRI
April 15, 2002

C.Lisse,M.Mumm
D.M.Kim,K.W.Paik,J.Eaglhauser,MPE

Total Steps

STEP 1.   Making a New Image

STEP 2.   Making a Cloud-Shaped Texture

STEP 3.   Enhancing and Inverting the Cloud Texture

STEP 4.   Emphasizing Dark Tones in the Cloud Texture

STEP 5.   Softening the Cloud Texture

STEP 6.   Applying Dimensional Lighting to Create a Rocky Texture

STEP 7.   Adding a Gradient Layer

STEP 8.   Blending the Gradient and the Rocky Surface

STEP 9.   Adding Noise to the Image

STEP 10. Drawing a Cross to Use as a Pattern

STEP 11. Saving the Pattern

STEP 12. Filling the Layer with the Pattern

STEP 13. Blending the Rocky Surface and the Cross Pattern

STEP 14. Adding Text to Complete the Image

STEP 1. Making a New Image

Choose File, New (Ctrl/Command+N) from the menu bar to open the New dialog box. Set the Width to 800 pixels and the Height to 500 pixels. Set the Resolution to 150 pixels/inch, make sure that White is selected under Contents, and click OK to create a new image.

STEP 2. Making a Cloud-Shaped Texture

Click the Default Foreground and Background Colors button on the toolbox to make the foreground color black and the background color white. Choose Filter, Render, Clouds from the menu bar to fill the Background layer with a cloud texture.

STEP 3. Enhancing and Inverting the Cloud Texture

Choose Filter, Render, Difference Clouds from the menu bar to create a more complex texture. Choose Image, Adjustments, Invert (Ctrl/Command+I) to invert the image colors. A pattern of irregular white lines emerges in the image.

STEP 4. Emphasizing Dark Tones in the Cloud Texture

Choose Image, Adjustments, Curves (Ctrl/Command+M) from the menu bar. In the Curves dialog box, bend the curve into the shape shown here. To do so, click the diagonal line to create a point on the curve, and then drag it into position. Click OK to apply the changes and emphasize the dark regions of the image.

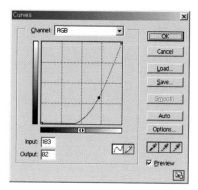

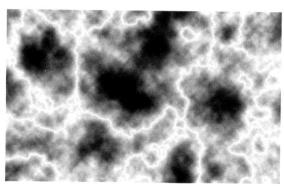

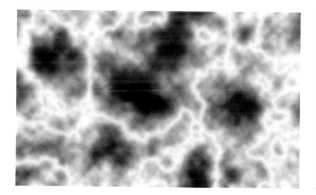

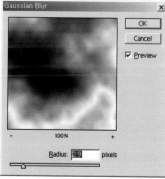

STEP 5. Softening the Cloud Texture

Choose Filter, Blur, Gaussian Blur from the menu bar to open the Gaussian Blur dialog box. Set the Radius to 2.9, and then click OK to soften the texture.

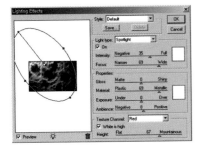

STEP 6. Applying Dimensional Lighting to Create a Rocky Texture

Choose Filter, Rendering, Lighting Effects to open the Lighting Effects dialog box. Adjust the handles in the Preview area as shown here to redirect the "light" to shine from the upper-left corner. Choose Red, Green, or Blue from the Texture Channel drop-down list. Click OK to apply the changes to the image. The texture now resembles the rocky surface of a planet.

STEP 7. Adding a Gradient Layer

Click the Create a new layer button (Shift+Ctrl/Command+N) on the Layers palette to add a new layer named Layer 1. Click the Switch Foreground and Background Colors button on the toolbox to set the foreground color to white and the background color to black. Choose the Gradient tool from the toolbox, and then click the Radial Gradient button on the Options bar. Drag from the upper-left corner to the lower-right corner of the image as shown here to add the gradient to the layer.

STEP 8. Blending the Gradient and the Rocky Surface

With Layer 1 still selected in the Layers palette, open the Layer Style drop-down list from the upper-left corner of the Layers palette, and then click Multiply. Also use the Opacity slider on the Layers palette to change the layer's Opacity setting to 35%.

STEP 9. Adding Noise to the Image

Click the palette menu button in the upper-right corner of the Layers palette, and then click Merge Down to merge both layers to the Background layer. Choose

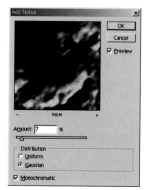

Filter, Noise, Add Noise from the menu bar to open the Add Noise dialog box. Click the Monochromatic check box to check it, set the Amount to 7, and then click OK to add a bit of graininess to the image.

STEP 10. Drawing a Cross to Use as a Pattern

Click the Create a new layer button (Shift+Ctrl/Command+N) on the Layers palette to add a new layer named Layer 1. Click the Default Foreground and Background Colors button on the toolbox to set the foreground color to black, and then use the Paint Bucket tool or press Alt/Option+Del to fill Layer 1 with black. Use the Zoom tool to magnify the image to the highest zoom

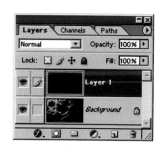
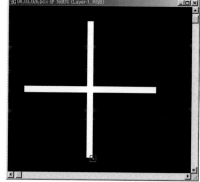

(1600%). Click the Switch Foreground and Background Colors button on the toolbox to set the foreground color to white. Choose the Pencil tool from the toolbox. Click the Click to open the Brush Preset picker button on the Options bar, drag the Master Diameter slider to set the brush size to 1 px, and then click the Click to open the Brush Preset picker button again to close the preset picker. Then draw a cross in the image window as shown here.

STEP 11. Saving the Pattern

Use the Navigator palette to zoom out to 100% size and view the image so that the cross appears in the upper-left corner of the image window. Choose the Rectangular Marquee tool from the toolbox, and then drag to make a square selection frame with ample space below and to the right of the cross, as shown here. Press and hold the Shift key while you drag to select a perfect square. Choose Edit, Define Pattern to open the Pattern Name dialog box. Enter a Name for the pattern, if desired, and then click OK to save the pattern. Choose Select, Deselect (Ctrl/Command+D) from the menu bar to remove the selection marquee.

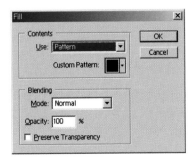

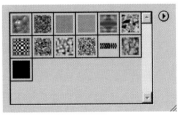

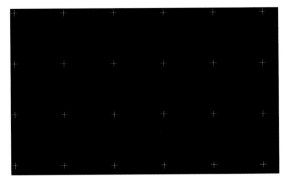

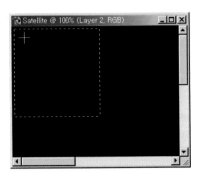

STEP 12. Filling the Layer with the Pattern

With the Layer 1 layer still selected in the Layers palette, choose Edit, Fill from the menu bar to open the Fill dialog box. Choose Pattern from the Use drop-down list, and then click the Custom Pattern box to open a palette of available patterns. Double-click the pattern you saved in Step 11, and then click OK to fill Layer 1 with the new pattern.

STEP 13. Blending the Rocky Surface and the Cross Pattern

With Layer 1 still selected in the Layers palette, open the Layer Style drop-down list from the upper-left corner of the Layers palette, and then click Difference. The cross pattern, which looks like coordinate points, appear in an inverted color.

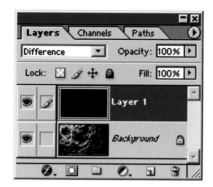

Comet Hyakutake, C/1996 B2   ROSAT HRI

April 15, 2002

+
nucleus

C.Lisse,M.Mumma,Nasa PED
D.M.Kim,K.W.Paik,J.Eaglhauser,MPE

STEP 14. Adding Text to Complete the Image

Use the Horizontal Type tool and Character palette to add text in a font resembling typewriter type (such as Courier New) as shown here to complete this image.

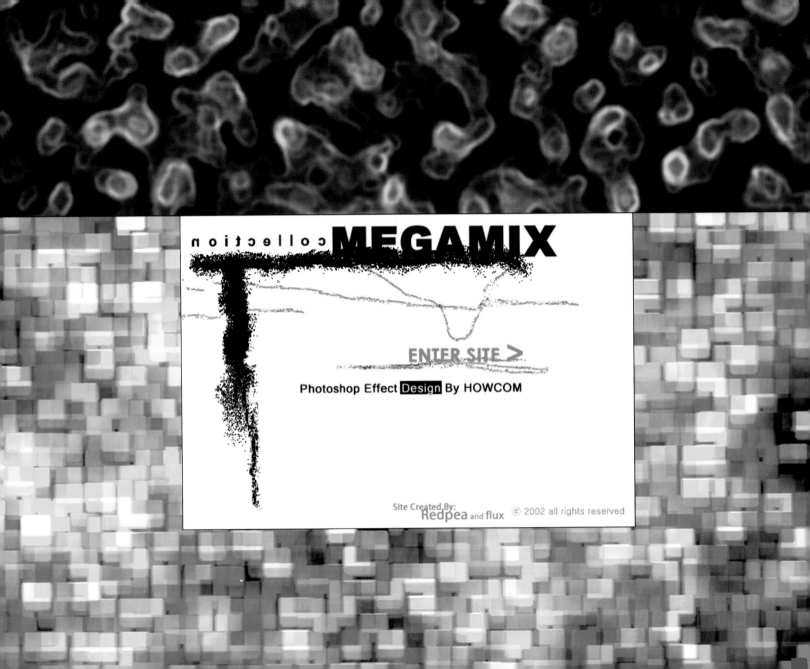

collection **MEGAMIX**

ENTER SITE >

Photoshop Effect Design By HOWCOM

Site Created By:
Redpea and flux © 2002 all rights reserved

Project 17: Charcoal Drawing

Use the Displace filter to create an image that appears to have been hand-drawn with charcoal.

Charcoal Drawing

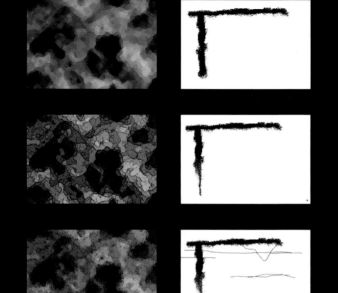

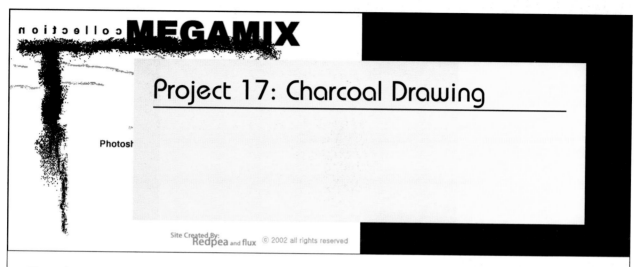

Project 17: Charcoal Drawing

Total Steps

STEP 1.   Making a New Image

STEP 2.   Adding a Cloud Texture

STEP 3.   Applying the Palette Knife Filter to the Cloud Texture

STEP 4.   Adding Edges to the Texture

STEP 5.   Saving the Displace Map File

STEP 6.   Making a New Image

STEP 7.   Filling the Selection to Create Black Lines

STEP 8.   Applying the Displace Filter

STEP 9.   Adding Detail to the Texture

STEP 10. Adding Graininess to an Area

STEP 11. Adding Flowing Effects to the Texture

STEP 12. Applying the Displace Filter Again

STEP 13. Adding Pencil Lines

STEP 14. Completing the Image

STEP 1. Making a New Image

Choose File, New (Ctrl/Command+N) from the menu bar to open the New dialog box. Set the Width to 800 pixels and the Height to 600 pixels. Set the Resolution to 150 pixels/inch, make sure that White is selected under Contents, and click OK to create a new image. You'll use this image to create a displace map file for use later in this project.

STEP 2. Adding a Cloud Texture

Click the Default Foreground and Background Colors button on the toolbox to make the foreground color black and the background color white. Choose Filter, Render, Clouds from the menu bar to fill the Background layer with a cloud texture. Choose Filter, Render, Difference Clouds to further blend the cloud texture.

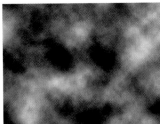

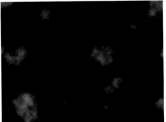

STEP 3. Applying the Palette Knife Filter to the Cloud Texture

Choose Image, Adjustments, Invert (Ctrl/Command+I) from the menu bar to invert the image colors. Choose Filter, Artistic, Palette Knife from the menu bar to open the Palette Knife dialog box. Choose the settings shown here, and then click OK to give the cloud texture a mottled appearance.

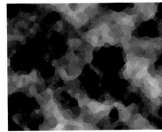

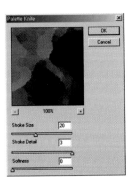

STEP 4. Adding Edges to the Texture

Choose Filter, Artistic, Poster Edges from the menu bar to open the Poster Edges dialog box. Choose the settings shown here, and then click OK to add rough, black edges to the shapes in the texture.

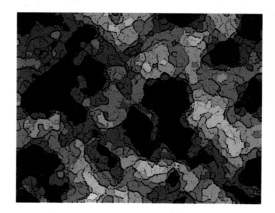

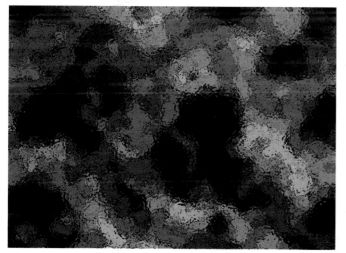

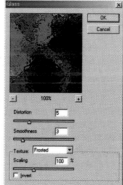

STEP 5. Saving the Displace Map File

Choose Filter, Distort, Glass to open the Glass dialog box. Choose the settings shown here, and then click OK to give the texture a glassy appearance. Now save this file for use as the displace map. Choose File, Save (Ctrl/Command+S) from the menu bar, and then use the Save As dialog box to save this file as a Photoshop file named Displace.psd. For your convenience, you can instead use the source file offered on the supplementary CD-ROM (Book\Sources\Displace.psd). Close the file that you've created.

STEP 6. Making a New Image

Choose File, New (Ctrl/Command+N) from the menu bar to open the New dialog box. Set the Width to 600 pixels and the Height to 400 pixels. Set the Resolution to 150 pixels/inch, make sure that White is selected under Contents, and click OK to create a new image. Choose the Rectangular Marquee tool, and make the selections shown here. After you select the first rectangle, press and hold the Shift key to select the second rectangular area.

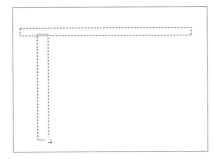

STEP 8. Applying the Displace Filter

Choose Filter, Distort, Displace from the menu bar to open the Displace dialog box. Choose the settings shown here, and then click OK. Use the Choose a displacement map dialog box that appears to select the Photoshop (Displace.psd) file you saved in Step 4, or the Displace.psd file from the supplementary CD-ROM. Click Open to transform the lines using the displace map file.

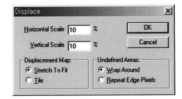

STEP 7. Filling the Selection to Create Black Lines

Click the Create a new layer button (Shift+Ctrl/Command+N) on the Layers palette to add a new layer named Layer 1. Click the Default Foreground and Background Colors button on the toolbox to set the foreground color to black, and then use the Paint Bucket tool or press Alt/Option+Del to fill the selection with black. Choose Select, Deselect (Ctrl/Command+D) from the menu bar to remove the selection marquee.

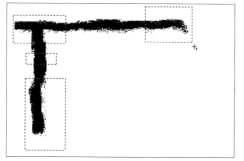

STEP 9. Adding Detail to the Texture

Choose the Rectangular Marquee tool from the toolbox, and drag to select areas to emphasize, as shown here. After you select the first rectangle, press and hold the Shift key while dragging to select additional areas. Choose Filter, Distort, Displace from the menu bar to open the Displace dialog box. Click the Tile option under Displacement Map, and then click OK. Use the Choose a displacement map dialog box that appears to select the Photoshop (Displace.psd) file you saved in Step 4, or the Displace.psd file from the supplementary CD-ROM. Click Open to add more detail to the texture in the selected areas. Choose Select, Deselect (Ctrl/Command+D) from the menu bar to remove the selection marquee.

STEP 10. Adding Graininess to an Area

With Layer 1 still selected, click the Add a layer mask button on the Layers palette to add a layer mask to the layer. Click the Switch Foreground and Background Colors button in the toolbox to make the foreground color black and the background color white. Choose the Gradient tool from the toolbox, click the Linear Gradient button on the Options bar, and drag from the bottom to the center of the image to add a gradient to the mask, fading the bottom of the vertical black line. With Layer 1 still selected in the Layers palette, open the Layer Style drop-down list from the upper-left corner of the Layers palette, and then click Dissolve. The black lines become very grainy in appearance.

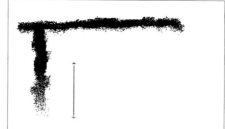

STEP 11. Adding Flowing Effects to the Texture

Click the Create a new layer button (Shift+Ctrl/Command+N) on the Layers palette to add a new layer named Layer 2. With the foreground color still set to black, choose the Brush tool from the toolbox. Click the Click to open the Brush Preset picker button on the Options bar, choose a hard round brush shape, drag the Master Diameter slider to set the brush size to 5, and then click the Click to open the Brush Preset picker button again to close the preset picker. Then draw flowing lines at the bottom of the vertical line as shown here.

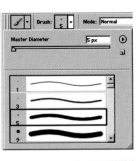

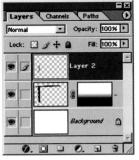

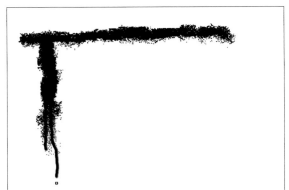

STEP 12. Applying the Displace Filter Again

With Layer 2 still selected in the Layers palette, choose Filter, Distort, Displace from the menu bar to open the Displace dialog box. Choose the settings shown here, and then click OK. Use the Choose a displacement map dialog box that appears to select the Photoshop (Displace.psd) file you saved in Step 4, or the Displace.psd file from the supplementary CD-ROM. Click Open to transform the flowing lines on the layer using the displace map file.

STEP 13. Adding Pencil Lines

Click the Create a new layer button (Shift+Ctrl/Command+N) on the Layers palette to add a new layer named Layer 3. Choose the Pencil tool from the toolbox. Click the Click to open the Brush Preset picker button on the Options bar, drag the Master Diameter slider to set the brush size to 1 px, and then click the Click to open the Brush Preset picker button again to close the preset picker. Then draw lines on the image as shown here.

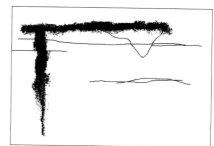

STEP 14. Completing the Image

With Layer 2 still selected in the Layers palette, choose Filter, Distort, Displace from the menu bar to open the Displace dialog box. Choose the settings shown here, and then click OK. Use the Choose a displacement map dialog box that appears to select the Photoshop (Displace.psd) file you saved in Step 4, or the Displace.psd file from the supplementary CD-ROM. Click Open to make the lines on Layer 3 look like they have been drawn using an actual pencil. Use the Horizontal Type tool and Character palette to add text in various styles as shown here. Flip the word "collection" at the top of the image using the Edit, Transform, Flip Horizontal command.

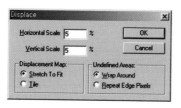
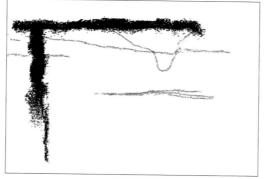

Project 18: Spring Breeze

In this project, create an image that looks like a soft watercolor painting of grass blowing in a spring breeze. Use a simple effect to blend the text into the watercolor image to enhance the overall effect.

PED Photoshop Effect Design

Spring Breeze

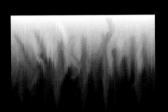

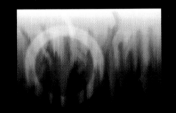

PED Photoshop Effect Design

Project 18: Spring Breeze

PED Photoshop Effect Design

Total Steps

STEP 1. Creating a New Image with a Gradient Background

STEP 2. Using the Smudge Tool to Make Blades of Grass

STEP 3. Simulating the Wind

STEP 4. Adding Color to the Grass

STEP 5. Adding Guidelines to the Image

STEP 6. Selecting a Donut Shape

STEP 7. Filling the Donut

STEP 8. Softening the Donut

STEP 9. Adding a 5 to the Image

STEP 10. Making the 5 Transparent

STEP 11. Adding More Text

STEP 12. Adding Shadows to the Text

STEP 13. Adding a Layer to Blur Text

STEP 14. Sizing the Black Motion Text

STEP 15. Bending the Black Motion Text

STEP 16. Blending the Black Motion Text

STEP 17. Adding the Remaining Text

STEP 1. Creating a New Image with a Gradient Background

Choose File, New (Ctrl/Command+N) from the menu bar to open the New dialog box. Set the Width to 800 pixels and the Height to 600 pixels. Set the Resolution to 150 pixels/inch, make sure that White is selected under Contents, and click OK to create a new image. Click the Default Foreground and Background Colors button on the toolbox to set the foreground color to black and the background color to white. Choose the Gradient tool from the toolbox, and then click the Linear Gradient button on the Options bar. Drag from the bottom to the top of the image window to create the gradient shown here on the Background Layer.

STEP 2. Using the Smudge Tool to Make Blades of Grass

Choose the Smudge tool from the toolbox. Click the Click to open the Brush Preset picker button on the Options bar, scroll down the list of available brushes, and then click the Chalk 36 pixels brush. Drag the Master Diameter slider to set the brush size to 46 px, and then click the Click to open the Brush Preset picker button again to close the preset picker. Change the Strength setting on the Options bar to 75%, and then drag vertically (from bottom to top) on the image to simulate blades of grass, as shown here.

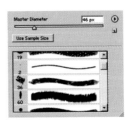 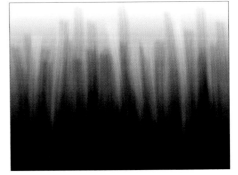

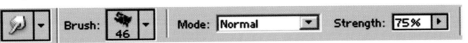

STEP 3. Simulating the Wind

Click the Click to open the Brush Preset picker button on the Options bar, drag the Master Diameter slider to set the brush size to 12 px, and then click the Click to open the Brush Preset picker button again to close the preset picker. With the Smudge tool still selected, drag in S shapes (from the bottom up) to make the blades of grass appear to be blowing in the wind.

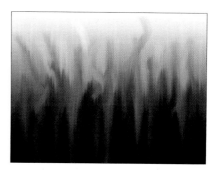

STEP 4. Adding Color to the Grass

Click the Create a new layer button (Shift+Ctrl/Command+N) on the Layers palette to add a new layer named Layer 3. Use the Color palette to set the foreground color to a dark yellow green (R:81, G:121, B:55). Use the Paint Bucket tool or press Alt/Option+Del to fill Layer 1 with green. With Layer 1 still selected in the Layers palette, open the Layer Style drop-down list from the upper-left corner of the Layers palette, and then click Overlay to mix the colors of the two layers evenly, making the blades of grass green.

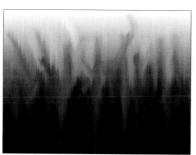

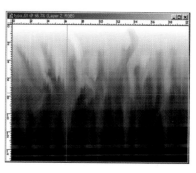

STEP 5. Adding Guidelines to the Image

Choose View, Rulers (Ctrl/Command+R) to display rulers in the image window. Drag down from the horizontal ruler and right from the vertical ruler to add guidelines to the image as shown here.

STEP 6. Selecting a Donut Shape

Click the Create a new layer button (Shift+Ctrl/Command+N) on the Layers palette to add a new layer named Layer 2. Choose the Elliptical Marquee tool from the toolbox. Move the crosshair pointer over the intersection of the guidelines, press and hold Shift+Alt/Option, and drag out to the size you want for the outer boundary of the donut. Move the crosshair over the intersection of the guidelines again, press and hold the Alt/Option key only, and then start dragging. Release the Alt/Option key, press and hold Shift+Alt/Option again, and continue dragging to draw the inner boundary of the donut. This latter technique subtracts the area within the inner circle from the selection.

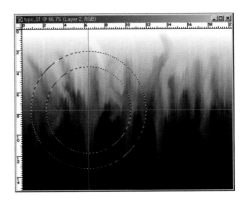

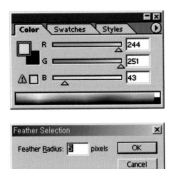

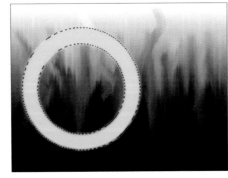

STEP 7. Filling the Donut

Choose Select, Feather from the menu bar to open the Feather Selection dialog box, set the Feather Radius to 5, and then click OK to soften the boundaries of the selection. Use the Color palette to set the foreground color to yellow (R:244, G:251, B:43), and then use the Paint Bucket tool or press Alt/Option+Del to fill the selection with yellow. Choose View, Show, Guides (Ctrl/Command+;) from the menu bar to hide the guidelines. Choose Select, Deselect (Ctrl/Command+D) from the menu bar to remove the selection marquee.

STEP 8. Softening the Donut

Alt/Option-click the boundary between Layer 2 and Layer 1 in the Layers palette to group these two layers. The blend mode applied to Layer 1 now applies to Layer 2, as well. With Layer 2 still selected, use the Opacity slider on the Layers palette to change the Opacity setting for Layer 2 to 55%.

  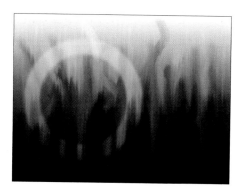

STEP 9. Adding a 5 to the Image

Choose the Horizontal Type tool from the toolbox, click the Toggle the Character and Paragraph palettes button to open the Character palette if needed, and then use the Character palette to choose a font and font size. Click in the center of the donut, type "5," and then click the Commit any current edits button on the Options bar to finish adding the 5. Choose Edit,

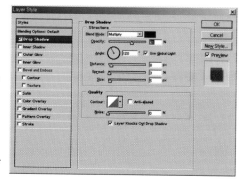 

Free Transform (Ctrl/Command+T) from the menu bar, drag the handles to adjust the size and position of the 5, and then press Enter/Return to finish the transformation. With the 5 layer still selected in the Layers palette, click the Add a layer style button on the Layers palette, and then click Drop Shadow. Specify the settings shown here in the Layer Style dialog box, and then click OK to add a drop shadow to the 5.

STEP 10. Making the 5 Transparent

Alt/Option-click the boundary between the 5 layer and Layer 2 in the Layers palette to group these two layers. With the 5 layer still selected, use the Opacity slider on the Layers palette to change the Opacity setting for Layer 2 to 44%. The blades of grass show through the number.

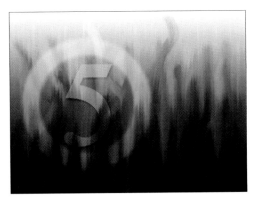

STEP 11. Adding More Text

Next, add the words "Text," "Motion," and "Graphics," each on its own layer. With the Horizontal Type tool still selected, drag on the image to add a layer for and define a position for the first word. (Drag away from any other text on the current layer to be sure to define a new text area rather than selecting the existing text.) Adjust the Character palette settings as shown on the left here, type "Text," and click the Commit any current edits button on the Options bar. Repeat the process using the additional Character palette settings shown here to add the other two words on separate text layers, varying the size of individual letters, if you prefer.

STEP 12. Adding Shadows to the Text

Click each new text layer in the Layers palette, click the Add a layer style button on the Layers palette, click Drop Shadow, and then click OK in the Layer Style dialog box to add a drop shadow to the text on the layer. Then, choose the Move tool from the toolbox, and drag the text on each of the new text layers to the positions shown here.

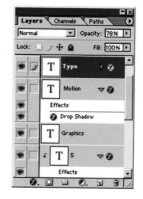

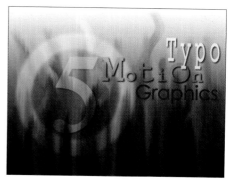

STEP 13. Adding a Layer to Blur Text

Click the Graphics layer in the Layers palette to select that layer, and then click the Create a new layer button (Shift+Ctrl/Command+N) on the Layers palette to add a new layer named Layer 3. Ctrl/Command-click the Motion layer in the Layers palette to make a selection in the shape of the letters. Click the Default Foreground and Background Colors button on the toolbox, and then use the Paint Bucket tool or press Alt/Option+Del to fill the selection with black. Choose Select, Deselect (Ctrl/Command+D) from the menu bar to remove the selection marquee. Choose Filter, Blur, Gaussian Blur from the menu bar to open the Gaussian Blur dialog box. Set the Radius to 1.8, and then click OK to create a blurred version of the Motion text on the layer.

STEP 14. Sizing the Black Motion Text

With Layer 3 still selected in the Layers palette, choose Edit, Transform, Scale in the menu bar. Drag the handles to resize the text as shown here, and then press Enter/Return to finish the transformation.

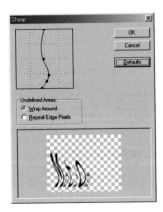

STEP 15. Bending the Black Motion Text

With Layer 3 still selected in the Layers palette, choose Filter, Distort, Shear from the menu bar to open the Shear dialog box. Create the curve shown at the top of the dialog box here by clicking to add points to the vertical line and then dragging those points into position. Click OK to apply the curves to the text.

STEP 16. Blending the Black Motion Text

In the Layers palette, drag Layer 3 down to place it above Layer 1 (the green layer). Photoshop automatically groups Layer 3 with Layer 1 (because you moved Layer 3 in between two grouped layers), so the layer effects of the lower Layer 1 layer apply to Layer 3. The text on Layer 3 resembles heat waves given off by the bed of grass.

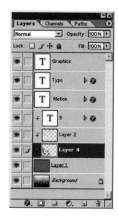

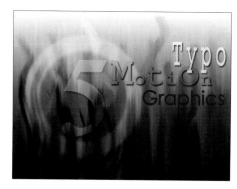

STEP 17. Adding the Remaining Text

Click the Create a new layer button (Shift+Ctrl/Command+N) in the Layers palette to add a layer named Layer 4. Drag Layer 4 to the top of the Layers palette. Choose the Horizontal Type tool from the toolbox, adjust the Character palette settings as shown here, and then click in the lower-left corner of the image and type "PED Photoshop Effect Design."

Click the Commit any current edits button on the Options bar. With Layer 4 still selected in the Layers palette, click the Add a layer style button on the Layers palette, click Drop Shadow, and then click OK in the Layer Style dialog box to add a drop shadow to the text on the layer.

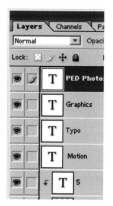

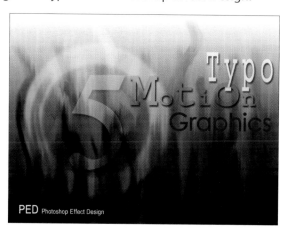

Project 19: Cubic Pipe

In this project, use various filters to create a dimensional pipe image. Using Photoshop, you can develop an image that is quite different from those made using 3-D graphics programs.

Cubic Pipe

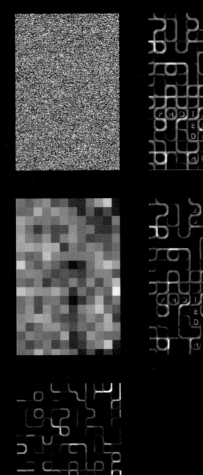

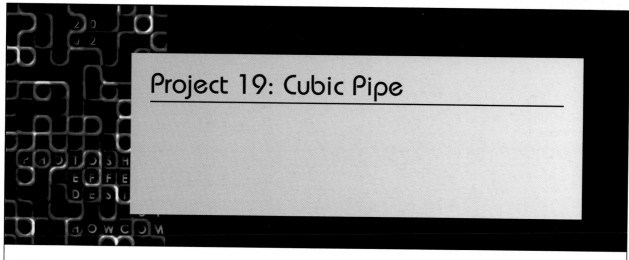

Project 19: Cubic Pipe

Total Steps

STEP 1. Making a New Image

STEP 2. Adding Noise to the Background Layer

STEP 3. Blurring the Speckles

STEP 4. Increasing the Noise Contrast

STEP 5. Adding a Mosaic Effect

STEP 6. Outlining the Blocks

STEP 7. Blurring the Edges

STEP 8. Emphasizing the Pipes with Directional Lighting

STEP 9. Brightening the Pipes

STEP 10. Scaling the Pipes

STEP 11. Adding a Black Background Layer

STEP 12. Changing the Color of the Pipes to Blue

STEP 13. Entering Evenly Spaced Text

STEP 14. Positioning Individual Letters

STEP 15. Inverting the Copied Image in the Pipe Layer

STEP 16. Making Black Pipes

STEP 17. Blurring the Black Pipes

STEP 18. Blending the Pipe Shadows

STEP 19. Modifying the Text Color to Complete the Image

STEP 1. Making a New Image

Choose File, New (Ctrl/Command+N) from the menu bar to open the New dialog box. Set the Width to 400 pixels and the Height to 600 pixels. Set the Resolution to 150 pixels/inch, make sure that White is selected under Contents, and click OK to create a new image.

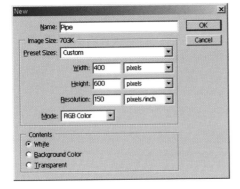

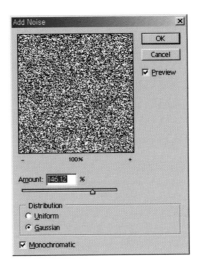

STEP 2. Adding Noise to the Background Layer

Choose Filter, Noise, Add Noise from the menu bar to open the Add Noise dialog box. Click the Monochromatic check box to check it. Set the Amount to 146, and then click OK to fill the Background layer with the black and white noise.

STEP 3. Blurring the Speckles

Choose Filter, Blur, Gaussian Blur from the menu bar to open the Gaussian Blur dialog box. Set the Radius to 5.2, and then click OK to blur the noise speckles together.

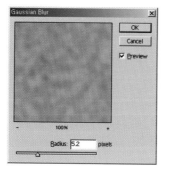

STEP 4. Increasing the Noise Contrast

Choose Image, Adjustments, Levels (Ctrl/Command+L) to open the Levels dialog box. Drag the Input Levels sliders to the center as shown here, and then click OK to create a sharp contrast between the black and white areas in the image.

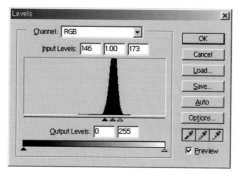

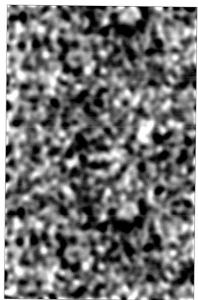

STEP 5. Adding a Mosaic Effect

Choose Filter, Pixelate, Mosaic from
the menu bar to open the Mosaic
dialog box. Set the Cell Size to 25,
and then click OK to cover the

Background
layer with a
mosaic of 25-
pixel squares.

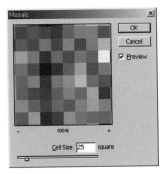

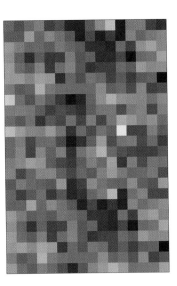

STEP 6. Outlining the Blocks

Choose Filter, Stylize, Glowing Edges from the menu bar.
Choose the settings shown here in the Glowing Edges
dialog box, and then click OK. Bright edges appear
around the mosaic blocks.

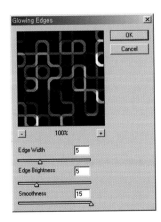

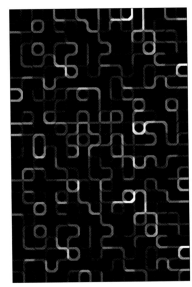

STEP 7. Blurring the Edges

Copy the Background layer by dragging it onto the Create a new layer button on the Layers palette. Choose Filter, Blur, Gaussian Blur to open the Gaussian Blur dialog box. Set the Radius to 1.5, and then click OK to blur the image.

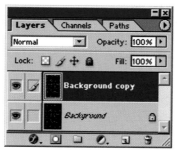

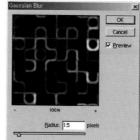

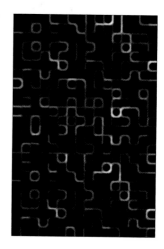

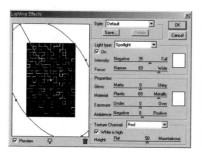

STEP 8. Emphasizing the Pipes with Directional Lighting

With the Background copy layer selected in the Layers palette, choose Filter, Render, Lighting Effects from the menu bar to open the Lighting Effects dialog box. Adjust the handles in the Preview area as shown here to redirect the "light" to shine from the upper-left corner. Choose Red from the Texture Channel drop-down list, and then click OK to apply the changes to the image, emphasizing the 3-D appearance of the pipes.

STEP 9. Brightening the Pipes

With the Background copy layer still selected in the Layers palette, open the Layer Style drop-down list from the upper-left corner of the Layers palette, and then click Screen to brighten the pipe image. Click the palette menu button in the upper-right corner of the Layers palette, and then click Merge Down to merge both layers onto the Background layer.

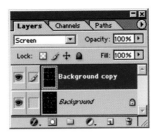

STEP 10. Scaling the Pipes

Use the Navigator palette to zoom the image to 50% size, so that you see some gray work area around the image in the image window. Choose the Rectangular Marquee tool from the toolbar, and then drag to select a portion of the image that your want to scale and use in the final composition. Choose Edit, Transform, Scale from the menu bar, press and hold the Shift key, drag to increase the size of the selection to fill the image canvas, and then press Enter/Return to finish the transformation. Selecting part of the image and scaling it to a larger size in this way makes the pipe grid appear larger.

STEP 11. Adding a Black Background Layer

Copy the Background layer by dragging it onto the Create a new layer button on the Layers palette. Click the Background layer in the Layers palette to select that layer. Click the Default Foreground and Background Colors button on the toolbox, and the use the Paint Bucket tool or press Alt/Option+Del to fill the Background layer with black. Click the Background copy layer in the Layers palette to select that layer.

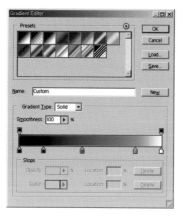

STEP 12. Changing the Color of the Pipes to Blue

Choose Image, Adjustments, Gradient Map from the menu bar to open the Gradient Map dialog box. Click the gradient in the Gradient Used for Grayscale Mapping box of the Gradient Map dialog box to open the Gradient Editor dialog box. Click the first gradient preset in the Presets area, and then create three more color stops at the bottom of the gradient preview to include additional gradient colors. To set up a stop, click the bottom of the gradient preview, and then use the Color box at the bottom of the dialog box to choose the color for that stop. Drag the far right color stop left to move it to the position shown here. (You can delete a color stop by dragging it down off the bottom of the preview.) Click OK to close the Gradient Editor dialog box, and then click OK again to apply the gradient.

STEP 13. Entering Evenly Spaced Text

Now add text, setting up the letters to fall within the pipes. Choose the Horizontal Type tool from the toolbox, click the Toggle the Character and Paragraph palettes button to open the Character palette if needed, and then use the Character palette to choose the settings shown here. Click the Right align

text button on the Options bar. Click to position the insertion point within the fifth full row between pipes at the right side of the image, and then type the five lines of text shown here, pressing Enter/Return after each line. Click the Commit any current edits button on the Options bar to finish adding the text. Choose the Move tool from the toolbox, and then drag the text on the layer so that it fits better within the boxes formed by the pipes, as shown here.

STEP 14. Moving Individual Letters

Even though adjusting the tracking or spacing between characters helped some letters better align vertically with the boxes formed by the pipes, you need to move other letters individually to align them. Right/Control-click the text layer in the Layers palette, and then click Rasterize Layer in the menu that appears. The vector text layer converts to a regular bitmap layer. Choose the Rectangular Marquee tool from the toolbox, drag over a letter to select it, choose the Move tool from the toolbox, and then press the ← and → arrow keys to position the letter. (Zoom in on the image to see your work in greater detail.) Repeat the process to position other letters. Choose Select, Deselect (Ctrl/Command+D) from the menu bar to remove the selection marquee after you position the last letter.

STEP 15. Inverting the Copied Image in the Pipe Layer

You want the letters to appear in the background and be hidden slightly by the pipe shadows. Copy the Background copy layer by dragging it onto the Create a new layer button on the Layers palette. With the new Background copy 2 layer still selected in the Layers palette, choose Image, Adjustments, Invert (Ctrl/Command+I) to invert the layer's colors. Next, choose Image, Adjustments, Desaturate (Shift+Ctrl/Command+U) to convert the layer to a black and white image. Drag the text layer below the Background copy layer in the Layers palette.

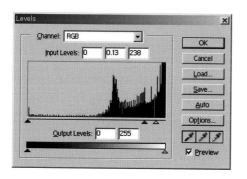

STEP 16. Making Black Pipes

With the Background copy 2 layer still selected in the Layers palette, choose Image, Adjustments, Levels (Ctrl/Command+L) from the menu bar to open the Levels dialog box. Drag the Input Levels sliders to the positions shown here, and then click OK to emphasize the black areas in the layer.

STEP 17. Blurring the Black Pipes

With the Background copy 2 layer still selected in the Layers palette, choose Filter, Blur, Gaussian Blur to open the Gaussian Blur dialog box. Set the Radius to 3, and then click OK to soften the black pipes.

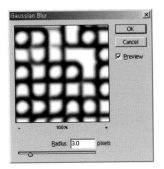

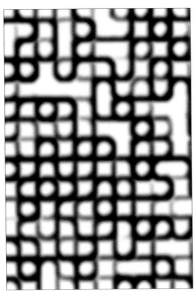

STEP 18. Blending the Pipe Shadows

Drag the Background copy 2 layer below the Background copy layer in the Layers palette. Click the Background copy layer in the Layers palette, open the Layer Style drop-down list from the upper-left corner of the Layers palette, and then click Screen. Click the Background copy 2 layer in the Layers palette, open the Layer Style drop-down list from the upper-left corner of the Layers palette, and then click Multiply. Choose the Move tool from the toolbox, and drag the Background copy layer slightly down and to the right to emphasize the shadows on the text.

STEP 19. Modifying the Text Color to Complete the Image

Click the text layer in the Layers palette to select that layer. Choose Image, Adjustments, Desaturate to convert the letters to gray. Choose the Rectangular Marquee tool from the toolbox, and drag to select a word or two of text to recolor. Choose Image, Adjustments, Hue/Saturation (Ctrl/Command+U) to open the Hue/Saturation dialog box. Click the Colorize check box to check it, drag the sliders to specify the settings shown here, and then click OK to apply the color to the selection. Choose Select, Deselect (Ctrl/Command+D) from the menu bar to remove the selection marquee.

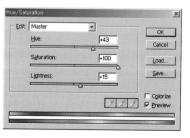

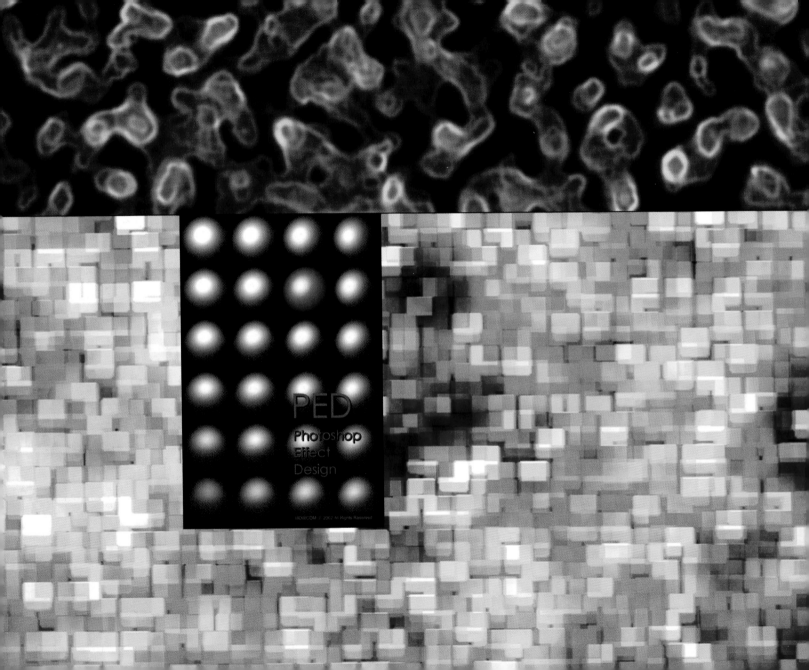

PED

Photoshop
Effect
Design

Project 20: 3-D Metallic Spheres

In this project, see how to use Photoshop to create strong 3-D objects that previously had to be made using a dedicated 3-D graphics program. The red sphere within the collection of 3-D metallic spheres brightens the entire image.

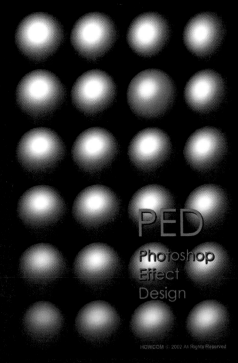

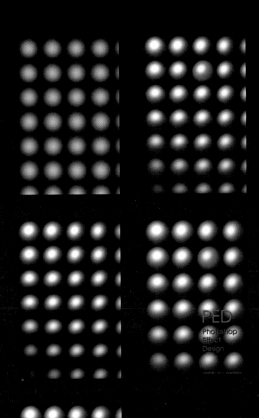

3-D Metallic Spheres

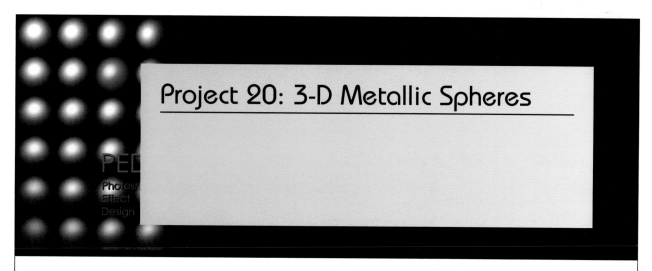

Project 20: 3-D Metallic Spheres

Total Steps

STEP 1. Making a New Image with a Black Background

STEP 2. Making a White Circle

STEP 3. Saving the Selection as an Alpha Channel

STEP 4. Using the Alpha Channel to Create a Sphere

STEP 5. Darkening the Sphere

STEP 6. Refining the Sphere Image

STEP 7. Saving the Sphere as a Pattern

STEP 8. Filling the New Image with the Sphere Pattern

STEP 9. Selecting the Black Areas between the Spheres

STEP 10. Copying the Layer and Deleting the Black Areas

STEP 11. Emphasizing the Spheres with Directional Lighting

STEP 12. Making the Spheres Look Metallic

STEP 13. Brightening the Metallic Spheres

STEP 14. Applying Shadows to the Metallic Spheres

STEP 15. Copying One Metallic Sphere

STEP 16. Making the Copied Sphere Red

STEP 17. Adding a Glow to the Red Sphere

STEP 18. Cutting the Image

STEP 19. Completing the Image

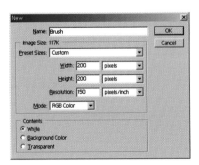

STEP 1. Making a New Image with a Black Background

Choose File, New (Ctrl/Command+N) from the menu bar to open the New dialog box. Set the Width and Height to 200 pixels. Set the Resolution to 150 pixels/inch, make sure that White is selected under Contents, and click OK to create a new image. Click the Default Foreground and Background Colors button on the toolbox to set the foreground color to black and the background color to white. Use the Paint Bucket tool or press Alt/Option+Del to fill the Background layer with black.

STEP 2. Making a White Circle

Choose the Elliptical Marquee tool from the toolbox. Press and hold the Shift key, and then drag on the image to draw a perfect circle. Click the Switch Foreground and Background Colors button on the toolbox to set the foreground color to white, and then use the Paint Bucket tool or press Alt/Option+Del to fill the selection with white.

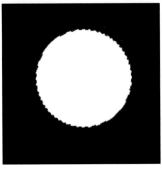

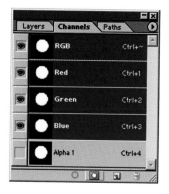

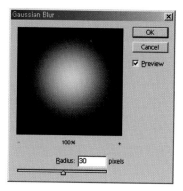

STEP 3. Saving the Selection as an Alpha Channel

Save the selection as an alpha channel so that you can reload the selection at any later time. Choose Window, Channels to open the Channels palette, and then click the Save selection as channel button on the palette. An alpha channel named Alpha 1 appears in the palette. Choose Select, Deselect (Ctrl/Command+D) from the menu bar to remove the selection marquee. Choose Filter, Blur, Gaussian Blur from the menu bar to open the Gaussian Blur dialog box. Set the Radius to 30, and then click OK to blur the circle image.

STEP 4. Using the Alpha Channel to Create a Sphere

Ctrl/command-click the Alpha 1 channel in the Channels palette to load the alpha channel as a selection. Choose Select, Inverse (Shift+Ctrl/Command+I) from the menu bar to invert the selection. With the

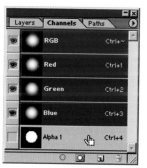

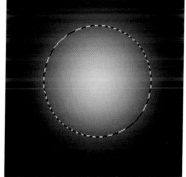

foreground color still set to white, press the Del key to delete the area in the selection, making it black. Choose Select, Deselect (Ctrl/Command+D) from the menu bar to remove the selection marquee.

STEP 5. Darkening the Sphere

Choose Window, Layers to redisplay the
Layers palette. Choose Image, Adjustments,
Curves (Ctrl/Command+M) from the menu bar.
In the Curves dialog box, bend the curve into
the shape shown here. To do so, click the
diagonal line to create a point on the curve,
and then drag it into position. Click OK to
apply the changes and emphasize the dark
areas of the sphere.

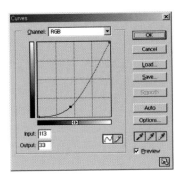

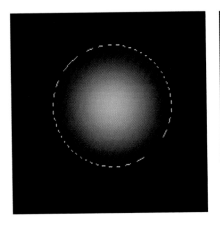

STEP 6. Refining the Sphere Image

Choose Window, Channels to return to the Channels
palette. Ctrl/Command-click the Alpha 1 channel to load
the channel as a selection. Choose Image, Crop from the
menu bar to crop the image to a tight size surrounding
the selection. Choose Select, Deselect (Ctrl/Command+D)
from the menu bar to remove the selection marquee.
Choose Window, Layers to redisplay the Layers palette.

STEP 7. Saving the Sphere as a Pattern

Choose Edit, Define Pattern from the menu bar to open the Pattern name dialog box. Type Ball as the pattern name, and then click OK to save the pattern. Close the image window. Choose File, New (Ctrl/Command+N) from the menu bar to open the New dialog box. Set the Width to 600 pixels and the Height to 800 pixels. Set the Resolution to 150 pixels/inch, make sure that White is selected under Contents, and click OK to create a new image.

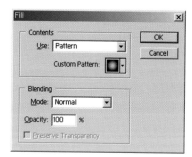

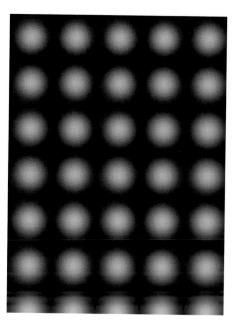

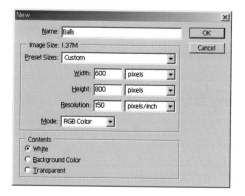

STEP 8. Filling the New Image with the Sphere Pattern

Choose Edit, Fill from the menu bar to open the Fill dialog box. Choose Pattern from the Use drop-down list, click on the Custom Pattern box to open a palette of patterns, and then double-click the Ball pattern you saved in Step 7. Click OK to fill the Background layer of the new image with the sphere pattern.

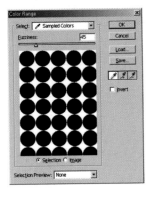

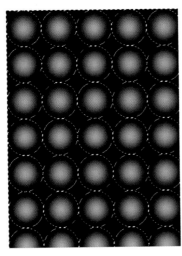

STEP 9. Selecting the Black Areas between the Spheres

Choose Select, Color Range to open the Color Range dialog box. Click a black area between spheres in the image window, change the Fuzziness setting in the dialog box to 45, and then click OK to select only the black background areas.

STEP 10. Copying the Layer and Deleting the Black Areas

Copy the Background layer by dragging it onto the Create a new layer button on the Layers palette. With the new Background copy layer still selected in the Layers palette, press the Del key to delete the selected black areas. Click the eye icon beside the Background layer in the Layers palette to hide that layer from view. After verifying the result, redisplay the Background layer by clicking the eye icon box beside the layer in the Layers palette. Choose Select, Deselect (Ctrl/Command+D) from the menu bar to remove the selection marquee.

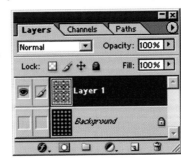

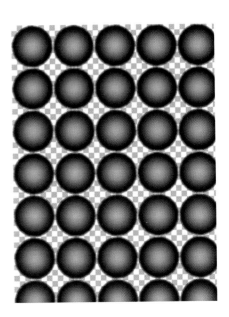

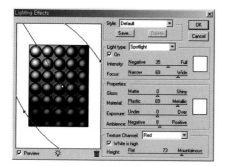

STEP 11. Emphasizing the Spheres with Directional Lighting

Click the Background copy layer in the Layers palette to select that layer. Choose Filter, Render, Lighting Effects from the menu bar to open the Lighting Effects dialog box. Adjust the handles in the Preview area as shown here to redirect the "light" to shine from the upper-left corner. Choose Red from the Texture Channel drop-down list, and then click OK to apply the changes to the image, emphasizing the 3-D appearance of the spheres.

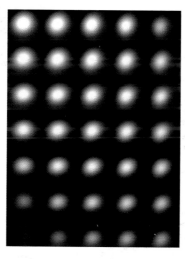

STEP 12. Making the Spheres Look Metallic

With the Background copy layer still selected in the Layers palette, choose Filter, Artistic, Palette Knife from the menu bar to open the Palette Knife dialog box. Choose the settings shown here, and then click OK. Leaving the Background copy layer selected, choose Filter, Noise, Median to open the Median dialog box. Set the Radius to 4, and then click OK.

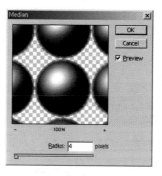

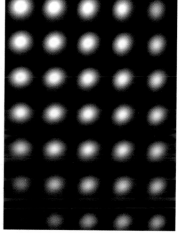

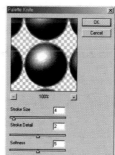

STEP 13. Brightening the Metallic Spheres

The metal spheres look too heavy. With the Background copy layer still selected in the Layers palette, choose Image, Adjustments, Levels (Ctrl/Command+L) from the menu bar to open the Levels dialog box. Drag the left Output levels slider to the position shown here, and then click OK to brighten the image, so the edges of the spheres become more apparent.

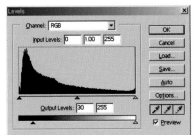

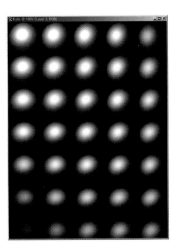

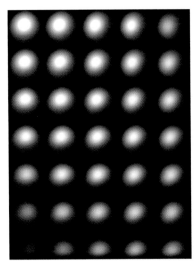

STEP 14. Applying Shadows to the Metallic Spheres

With the Background copy layer selected in the Layers palette, click the Add a layer style button on the palette, and then click Inner Shadow to open the Layer Style dialog box. Choose the settings shown here, and then click OK to emphasize the shadows on the lower-right areas of the spheres, opposite the light source.

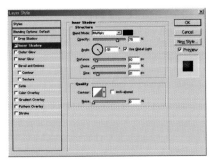

STEP 15. Copying One Metallic Sphere

Choose the Rectangular Marquee tool from the toolbox, and drag to select one of the spheres near the top of the image. Press Ctrl/Command+C to copy the selection, and then press Ctrl/Command+V to paste the selected metal sphere onto a new layer named Layer 1.

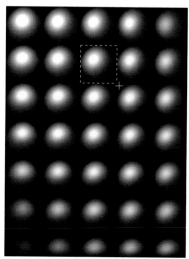

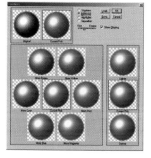

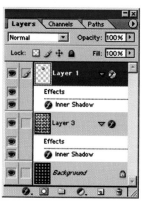

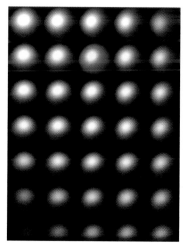

STEP 16. Making the Copied Sphere Red

Click the new Layer 1 layer in the Layers palette to select the layer, if needed. Choose Image, Adjustments, Variations from the menu bar to open the Variations dialog box. Click the More Red and More Yellow thumbnails as many times as needed until the sphere in the Current Pick thumbnail turns red. Click OK. In the Layers palette, drag the Inner Shadow effect from the Background copy layer to the Layer 1 layer to copy the inner shadow effect to the red sphere.

STEP 17. Adding a Glow to the Red Sphere

With the Layer 1 layer selected in the Layers palette, click the Add a layer style button on the palette, and then click Outer Glow. Choose the settings shown here in the Layer Style dialog box, and then click OK.

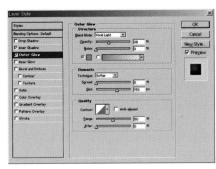

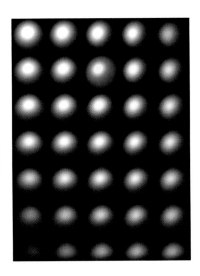

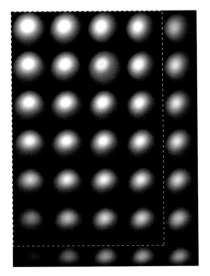

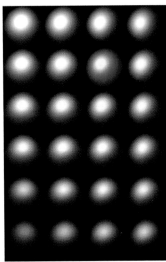

STEP 18. Cropping the Image

Choose the Rectangular Marquee tool from the toolbox, and then drag to select the desired portion, eliminating any partial spheres. Choose Image, Crop from the menu bar to remove areas outside the selection from the image. Choose Select, Deselect (Ctrl/Command+D) from the menu bar to remove the selection marquee.

STEP 19. Completing the Image

Use the Horizontal Type tool and the Character palette to add simple red text to the completed image. Also add a drop shadow to the text layer to emphasize the 3-D appearance of the image.

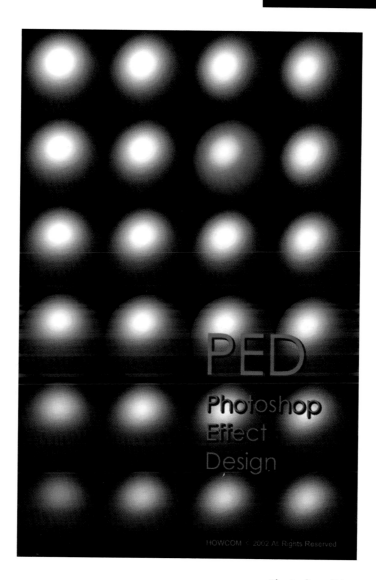

Project 21: Type Space

In this project, explore how to use Photoshop 7.0's new Pattern Maker to convert a portion of an image into a pattern. You'll create a pattern that looks like a snapshot of a rapidly moving object.

Type Space

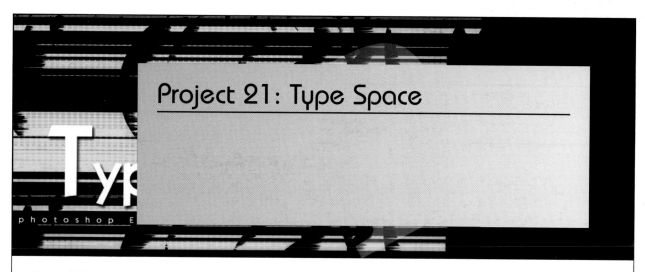

Project 21: Type Space

Total Steps

STEP 1. Making a New Image with a Cloud Texture Background

STEP 2. Applying the Paint Daub Filter

STEP 3. Adding an O

STEP 4. Making Three Rings

STEP 5. Merging and Copying Layers

STEP 6. Using the Pattern Maker Filter

STEP 7. Making a Stripe Pattern

STEP 8. Blending the Pattern Layers

STEP 9. Adding Wind

STEP 10. Adjusting the Stripe Layer Transparency

STEP 11. Creating a Pattern Image

STEP 12. Saving the Pattern

STEP 13. Applying the Pattern to a New Layer

STEP 14. Applying Directional Lighting to the Pattern Layer

STEP 15. Blending the Pattern Layer

STEP 16. Adding and Sizing Text

STEP 17. Adding an R

STEP 18. Adjusting the Text Transparency

STEP 19. Entering the Remaining Text

STEP 20. Adding a Shadow to the Typespace Layer to Complete the Image

STEP 1. Making a New Image with a Cloud Texture Background

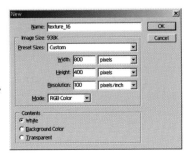

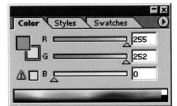

Choose File, New (Ctrl/Command+N) from the menu bar to open the New dialog box. Set the Width to 800 pixels and the Height to 400 pixels. Set the Resolution to 100 pixels/inch, make sure that White is selected under Contents, and click OK to create a new image. Use the Color palette to specify the foreground (R:251, G:102, B:3) and background (R:255, G:252, B:0) colors shown here. Choose Filter, Render, Clouds from the menu bar to fill the Background with a cloud texture mixing the foreground and background colors.

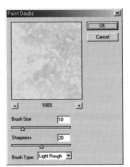

STEP 2. Applying the Paint Daub Filter

Choose Filter, Artistic, Paint Daubs from the menu bar to open the Paint Daubs dialog box. Choose the settings shown here, and then click OK to apply the filter to the Background texture.

STEP 3. Adding an O

Click the Default Foreground and Background Colors box on the toolbox to reset the foreground color to black. Choose the Horizontal Type tool from the toolbox, click the Toggle the Character and Paragraph palettes button to open the Character palette if needed, and then choose the settings shown here in the Character palette. Click on the image, type "O," and then click the Commit any current edits button on the Options bar to finish adding the letter.

STEP 4. Making Three Rings

With the new O layer selected in the Layers palette, choose Edit, Free Transform (Ctrl/Command+T) from the menu bar, drag the handles to increase the letter's size, and then press Enter/Return to finish the transformation. Right/Control-click the O layer in the Layers palette, and then click Rasterize Layer in the menu that appears. Ctrl/Command-click the O layer in the Layers palette to make a selection in the shape of the letter. Choose the Move tool from the toolbox, and press and hold the Alt/Option key while dragging the selection to make two copies of the shape on the same layer. Choose Select, Deselect (Ctrl/Command+D) from the menu bar to remove the selection marquee.

STEP 5. Merging and Copying Layers

Click the palette menu button in the upper-right corner of the Layers palette, and then click Merge Visible to merge the two layers to the Background layer. Copy the Background layer by dragging it onto the Create a new layer button on the Layers palette.

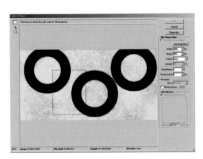
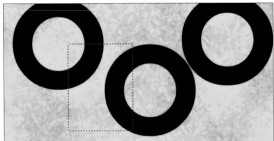

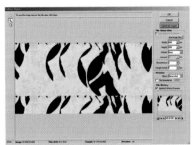

STEP 6. Using the Pattern Maker Filter

With the Background copy layer selected in the Layers palette, choose the Rectangular Marquee tool from the toolbox, and then drag to select an area that includes parts of two Os. Choose Filter, Pattern Maker from the menu bar to open the Pattern Maker dialog box. Under Tile Generation, set the Width to 800 and the Height to 300, and then click Generate. Click Generate Again until the pattern achieves the desired appearance, and then click OK to apply the pattern to the layer.

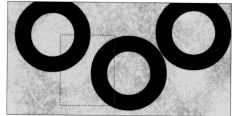

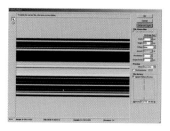

STEP 7. Making a Stripe Pattern

Click the eye icon beside the Background copy layer in the Layers palette to hide that layer, and then click the Background layer to select it. With the selection from the prior layer still active, choose Filter, Pattern Maker from the menu bar to open the Pattern Maker dialog box. Under Tile Generation, set the Width to 800 and the Height to 300, and then click Generate. Click the Generate Again button until the pattern achieves the desired appearance, and then click OK to apply the pattern to the layer, which is renamed Layer 0 in the process. Choose Select, Deselect (Ctrl/Command+D) from the menu bar to remove the selection marquee.

STEP 8. Blending the Pattern Layers

Double-click on the Layer 0 layer name in the Layers palette, type "Stripe," and then press Enter/Return to rename the layer. Click the Background copy layer in the Layers palette, open the Layer Style drop-down list from the upper-left corner of the Layers palette, and then click Darken.

STEP 9. Adding Wind

With the Background copy layer still selected in the Layers palette, choose Filter, Stylize, Wind from the menu bar to open the Wind dialog box. Choose the settings shown here, and then click OK to emphasize the sense of motion in the image.

STEP 10. Adjusting the Stripe Layer Transparency

Click the Stripe layer in the Layers palette to select that layer. Use the Fill slider on the Layers palette to change the layer's Fill setting to 88%.

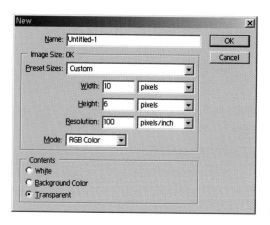

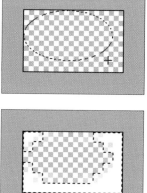

STEP 12. Saving the Pattern

Choose Edit, Define Pattern to open the Pattern Name dialog box. Enter a name for the pattern, if desired and then click OK to save the pattern. Close the image file you created to make the pattern, if desired.

STEP 11. Creating a Pattern Image

Choose File, New (Ctrl/Command+N) from the menu bar to open the New dialog box. Set the Width to 10 pixels and the Height to 6 pixels. Set the Resolution to 100 pixels/inch, click Transparent under Contents, and click OK to create a new image. After using the Zoom tool to zoom in on the image, choose the Elliptical Marquee tool from the toolbox. Drag in the image to create an ellipse, and then choose Select, Inverse (Shift+Ctrl/Command+I) to invert the selection. Click the Switch Foreground and Background Colors button on the toolbox to set the foreground color to white, and then use the Paint Bucket tool or press Alt/Option+Del to fill the selection with white. Choose Select, Deselect (Ctrl/Command+D) from the menu bar to remove the selection marquee.

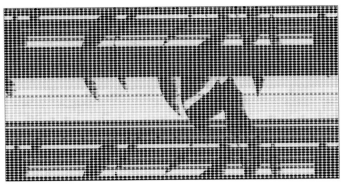

STEP 13. Applying the Pattern to a New Layer

Back in the project image file, click the Background copy layer in the Layers palette to select that layer. Click the Create a new layer button in the Layers palette to add a new layer named Layer 1. Choose Edit, Fill from the menu bar to open the Fill dialog box, and then click on the Custom Pattern box to open a palette of available patterns. Double-click the pattern you saved in Step 12, and then click OK to fill Layer 1 with the pattern.

STEP 14. Applying Directional Lighting to the Pattern Layer

With Layer 1 still selected in the Layers palette, choose Filter, Render, Lighting Effects to open the Lighting Effects dialog box. Adjust the handles in the Preview area as shown here to redirect the "light" to shine from the upper-left corner. Choose None from the Texture Channel drop-down list, and then click OK to apply the changes to the pattern.

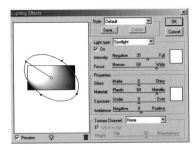

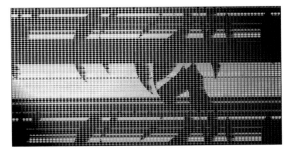

STEP 15. Blending the Pattern Layer

With Layer 1 still selected in the Layers palette, open the Layer Style drop-down list from the upper-left corner of the Layers palette, and then click Overlay.

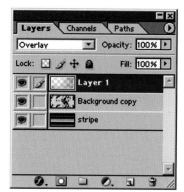

STEP 16. Adding and Sizing Text

Choose the Horizontal Type tool from the toolbox, and choose the settings shown here in the Character palette. Click in the image, and then type the text shown here. Use the Character palette to vary the font size of some letters to liven up the text, and then click the Commit any current edits button on the Options bar.

STEP 17. Adding an R

Click the Create a new layer button (Shift+Ctrl/Command+N) on the Layers palette to add a new layer named Layer 2. Choose the settings shown here in the Character palette, click in the image, type letter "R," and then click the Commit any current edits button on the Options bar. Choose Edit, Free Transform (Ctrl/Command+T) from the menu bar, drag the handles to adjust the size and rotation of the letter, and then press Enter/Return to finish the transformation.

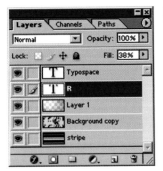

STEP 18. Adjusting the Text Transparency

Move the new R layer below the Typospace text layer in the Layers palette. With the R layer selected, use the Fill slider on the Layers palette to set the Fill value for the R layer to 38%.

STEP 19. Entering the Remaining Text

Click the Create a new layer button (Shift+Ctrl/Command+N) on the Layers palette to add a new layer named Layer 2. With the Horizontal Type tools still selected, choose the settings shown here in the Character palette. Click in the image window, type the remaining text shown here, and then click the Commit any current edits button on the Options bar.

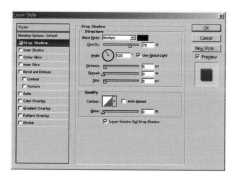

STEP 20. Adding a Shadow to the Typospace Layer to Complete the Image

Click the Typospace layer in the Layers palette to select that layer. Click the Add a layer style button on the Layers palette, click Drop Shadow, and then click OK in the Layer Style dialog box to complete the image.

214

PED

UNPLUGED

Texture Zone has a great ...tion of textures you can ...your Desktop, Website, ...evels or 3D art projects. ...here's also custom Desktops, ...cons and Animated Cursors. WebGfx is ready to use Web ...hics and WebCode shows ...some tricks to put it all ...er to make a slick site.

Project 22: Blue Distortion

Use the Displace filter to create an image that looks as if it has been casually drawn using blue charcoal.

Blue Distortion

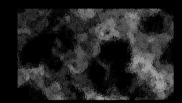

Project 22: Blue Distortion

Total Steps

STEP 1. Making a Selection in a New Image

STEP 2. Filling the Selection with Black

STEP 3. Applying the Displace Filter

STEP 4. Making a Selection in the Messy Image

STEP 5. Filling the Selection with Black

STEP 6. Displacing the New Rectangles

STEP 7. Cropping the Image

STEP 8. Merging the Layers

STEP 9. Making a Cloud Texture on a New Layer

STEP 10. Emphasizing the Cloud Texture

STEP 11. Making the Cloud Texture Blue

STEP 12. Applying Noise to a New Layer

STEP 13. Blending the Cloud and Noise Layers

STEP 14. Applying the Texture to the Messy Shapes

STEP 15. Adding the Title and Texture

STEP 16. Adding the Subtitles

STEP 17. Adding the Rest of the Text

STEP 18. Copying the Background Layer

STEP 19. Adding Horizontal Noise

STEP 20. Making the Noise Blue

STEP 21. Redisplaying the Image

STEP 1. Making a Selection in a New Image

Choose File, New (Ctrl/Command+N) from the menu bar to open the New dialog box. Set the Width to 800 pixels and the Height to 600 pixels. Set the Resolution to 150 pixels/inch, make sure that White is selected under Contents, and click OK to create a new image. Choose the Rectangular Marquee tool from the toolbox, and select a number of rectangles in the image. After you select the first rectangle, press and hold the Shift key to select additional rectangles.

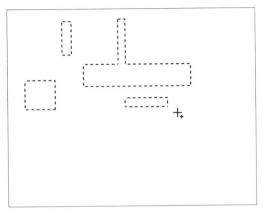

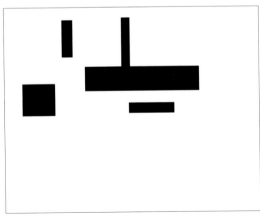

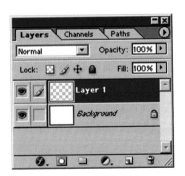

STEP 2. Filling the Selection with Black

Click the Create a new layer button (Shift+Ctrl/Command+N) on the Layers palette to add a new layer named Layer 1. Click the Default Foreground and Background Colors button on the toolbox to set the foreground color to black, and then use the Paint Bucket tool or press Alt/Option+Del to fill the selection with black. Choose Select, Deselect (Ctrl/Command+D) from the menu bar to remove the selection marquee.

STEP 3. Applying the Displace Filter

With the Layer 1 layer selected in the Layers palette, choose Filter, Distort, Displace from the menu bar to open the Displace dialog box. Choose the settings shown here, and then click OK. Use the Choose a displacement map dialog box that appears to select the \Book\Sources\Displace.psd file from the supplementary CD-ROM. Click Open to transform the rectangles using the displace map file.

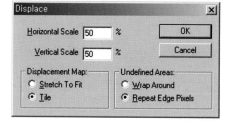

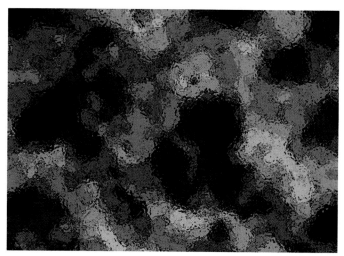

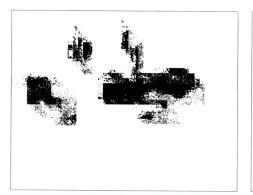

STEP 4. Making a Selection in the Messy Image

The image appears too sparse in certain areas. Choose the Rectangular Marquee tool from the toolbox, and then make several more rectangular selections. Press and hold the Shift key after selecting the first rectangle to select additional rectangles.

STEP 5. Filling the Selection with Black

Click the Create a new layer button
(Shift+Ctrl/Command+N) on the Layers palette to add
a new layer named Layer 2. With black still selected as
the foreground color, use the Paint Bucket tool or
press Alt/Option+Del to fill the selection with black.
Choose Select, Deselect (Ctrl/Command+D) from the
menu bar to remove the selection marquee. Click the
eye icon beside the Layer 1 layer in the Layers palette
to hide that layer.

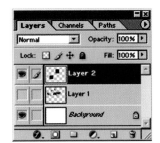

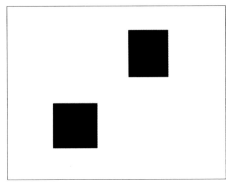

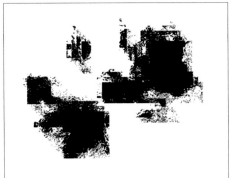

STEP 6. Displacing the New Rectangles

With the Layer 2 layer selected in the Layers palette, choose Filter, Distort, Displace from the menu bar to open the
Displace dialog box. Click OK, and then use the Choose a displacement map dialog box that appears to select the
\Book\Sources\Displace.psd file from the supplementary CD-ROM. Click Open to transform the rectangles using the
displace map file. Click the eye icon box beside the Layer 1 layer to redisplay the layer. Use the Move tool, if desired, to
arrange the textured rectangles on either layer.

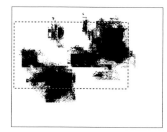   

STEP 7. Cropping the Image

Choose the Rectangular Marquee tool from the toolbox, and then drag on the image to select the area to use in the final composition. Choose Image, Crop to remove the areas outside the selection from the image. Choose Select, Deselect (Ctrl/Command+D) from the menu bar to remove the selection marquee.

STEP 8. Merging the Layers

With the Layer 2 layer selected in the Layers palette, click the palette menu button in the upper-right corner of the Layers palette, and then click Merge Down in the menu that appears to merge Layer 2 and Layer 1 into a single layer named Layer 1.

STEP 9. Making a Cloud Texture on a New Layer

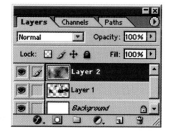

Click the Create a new layer button (Shift+Ctrl/Command+N) on the Layers palette to add a new layer named Layer 2. Click the Default Foreground and Background Colors button in the toolbox to make the foreground color black and the background color white. With the Layer 2 layer still selected in the Layers palette, choose Filter, Render, Clouds to fill the new layer with a cloud texture.

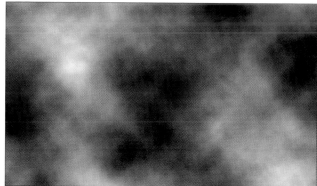

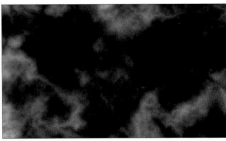

STEP 10. Emphasizing the Cloud Texture

With the Layer 2 layer still selected in the Layers palette, choose Filter, Render, Difference Clouds from the menu bar to adjust the cloud texture. Press Ctrl/Command+F to reapply the filter as needed until the texture reaches the desired appearance.

STEP 11. Making the Cloud Texture Blue

With the Layer 2 layer still selected in the Layers palette, choose Image, Adjustments, Gradient Map from the menu bar to open the Gradient Map dialog box. Click the gradient in the Gradient Used for Grayscale Mapping box of the Gradient Map dialog box to open the Gradient Editor dialog box. Click the first gradient preset in the Presets area,

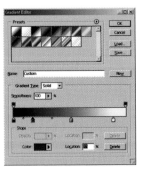

and then create two more color stops at the bottom of the gradient preview to include additional gradient colors. To set up a stop, click the bottom of the gradient preview, and then use the Color box at the bottom of the dialog box to choose the color for that stop. Drag the far right color stop left to move it to the position shown here. (You can delete a color stop by dragging it down off the bottom of the preview.) Click OK to close the Gradient Editor dialog box, and then click OK again to apply the gradient.

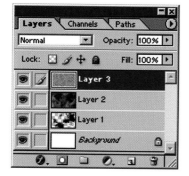

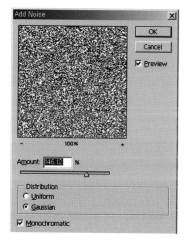

STEP 12. Applying Noise to a New Layer

Click the Create a new layer button (Shift+Ctrl/Command+N) on the Layers palette to add a new layer named Layer 3. Press Alt/Option+Del to fill the layer with the current background color, white. Choose Filter, Noise, Add Noise from the menu bar to open the Add Noise dialog box. Choose the Gaussian and Monochromatic Options as shown here, set the Amount to approximately 146, and then click OK to fill the layer with black and white noise.

STEP 13. Blending the Cloud and Noise Layers

With the Layer 3 layer still selected in the Layers palette, open the Layer Style drop-down list from the upper-left corner of the Layers palette, and then click Overlay. Also use the Opacity slider on the Layers palette to set the Opacity value for Layer 3 to 40%.

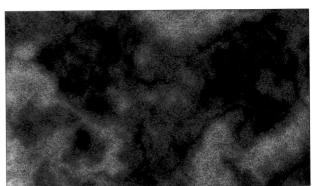

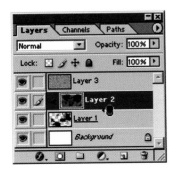

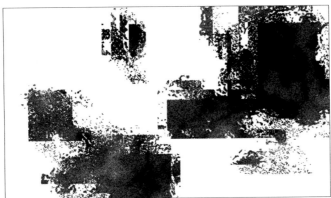

STEP 14. Applying the Texture to the Messy Shapes

In the Layers palette, Alt/Option-click the divider between the Layer 2 and Layer 1 layers to group the layers, applying the texture to the messy shapes.

 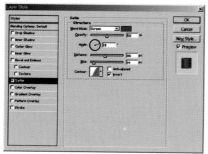  

STEP 15. Adding the Title and Texture

Choose the Horizontal Type tool from the toolbox, click the Toggle the Character and Paragraph palettes button to open the Character palette if needed, and then use the Character palette to choose the settings shown here. Click in the image window, type "PED," and then click the Commit any current edits button on the Options bar to finish the text. With the new PED layer selected in the Layers palette, click the Add a layer style button, and then click Satin. Choose the settings shown here in the Layer Style dialog box, and then click OK to apply a dark blue texture for the text.

STEP 16. Adding the Subtitles

Repeat the techniques in Step 15 to add the subtitles on separate layers, creating the layer to hold the text first, if needed. Rotate the number text using the Edit, Transform, Rotate 90° CW command. Also use the Move tool to move text into position on its layer, if needed.

STEP 17. Adding the Rest of the Text

Click the Create a new layer button (Shift+Ctrl/Command+N) on the Layers palette to add a new layer named Layer 4. Choose the Horizontal Type tool from the toolbox, choose an appropriate text color and choose other settings as desired in the Character palette, and then enter the text shown here. Click the Commit any current edits button on the Options bar to finish adding the text.

STEP 18. Copying the Background Layer

Add horizontal stripes to liven up the bland white background. Copy the Background layer by dragging it onto the Create a new layer button in the Layers palette. Click the eye icon beside all layers in the palette except the new Background copy layer to hide those layers from view.

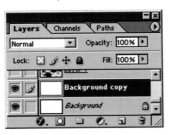

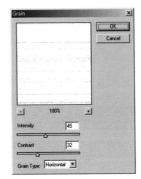

STEP 19. Adding Horizontal Noise

With the Background copy layer selected in the Layers palette, choose Filter, Texture, Grain from the menu bar to open the Grain dialog box. Choose the settings shown here, and then click OK to add black and white noise in horizontal lines across the image.

STEP 20. Making the Noise Blue

With the Background copy layer still selected in the Layers palette, choose Image, Adjustments, Hue/Saturation (Ctrl/Command+U) from the menu bar to open the Hue/Saturation dialog box. Click the Colorize check box to check it, drag the sliders to specify the settings shown here, and then click OK to apply a blue tone to the noise.

STEP 21. Redisplaying the Image

Click the eye icon box beside each of the hidden layers in the Layers palette to redisplay them.

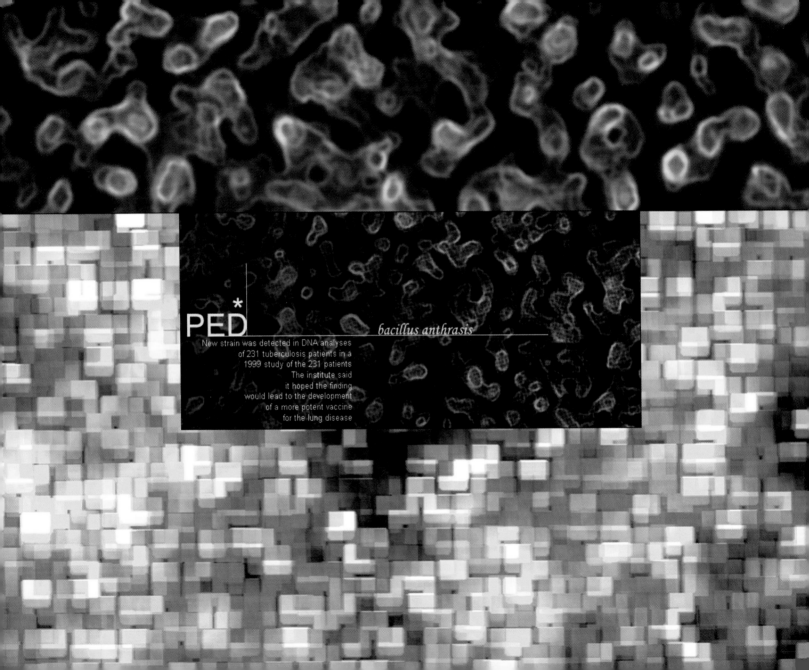

PED
*

bacillus anthrasis

New strain was detected in DNA analyses
of 231 tuberculosis patients in a
1999 study of the 231 patients
The institute said
it hoped the finding
would lead to the development
of a more potent vaccine
for the lung disease

Project 23: Bacteria Liquid

In this project, create an image of what appears to be a bacteria colony magnified under an electron microscope. The image looks like the light of an electron microscope illuminating the outline of the organisms floating through the liquid.

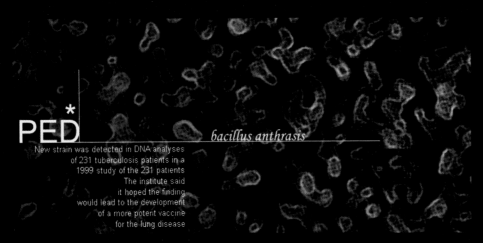

PED

*

bacillus anthrasis

New strain was detected in DNA analyses
of 231 tuberculosis patients in a
1999 study of the 231 patients
The institute said
it hoped the finding
would lead to the development
of a more potent vaccine
for the lung disease

Bacteria Liquid

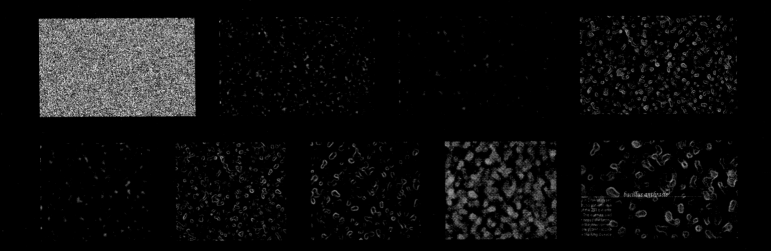

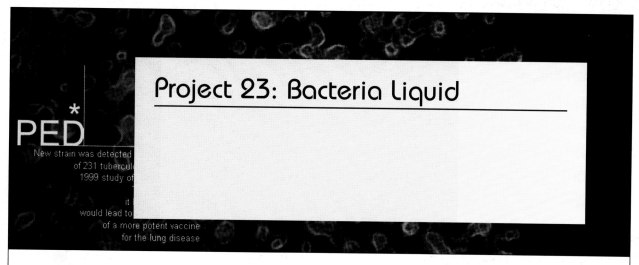

Project 23: Bacteria Liquid

New strain was detected
of 231 tubercul
1999 study of

it
would lead to
of a more potent vaccine
for the lung disease

Total Steps

STEP 1.   Adding Noise to a New Image
STEP 2.   Bunching the Noise Particles
STEP 3.   Making the Bacteria Outlines
STEP 4.   Detailing the Bacteria
STEP 5.   Blurring the Background Layer
STEP 6.   Blending the Bacteria Layer
STEP 7.   Adding Color to the Image
STEP 8.   Softening the Outline of
          the Bacteria
STEP 9.   Adding Color to the Bacteria
STEP 10. Redisplaying the Background
STEP 11. Doubling the Image Size

STEP 12. Adding Color to the
          Selected Bacteria
STEP 13. Adding Color to the Outlines of the
          Selected Bacteria
STEP 14. Merging the Layers
STEP 15. Sharpening the Background Layer
STEP 16. Coloring the Background Copy Layer
STEP 17. Blending the Layers
STEP 18. Cropping the Image
STEP 19. Adding a Gradient to a New Layer
STEP 20. Blending the Gradient
STEP 21. Completing the Image

STEP 1. Adding Noise to a New Image

Choose File, New (Ctrl/Command+N) from the menu bar to open the New dialog box. Set the Width to 800 pixels and the Height to 450 pixels. Set the Resolution to 150 pixels/inch, make sure that White is selected under Contents, and click OK to create a new image. Click the Default Foreground and Background Colors button on the toolbox to set the foreground color to black and the background color to white. Choose Filter, Noise, Add Noise from the menu bar to open the Add Noise dialog box. Specify the settings shown here, and then click OK to add the noise to the image.

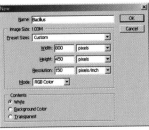

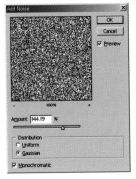

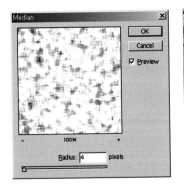

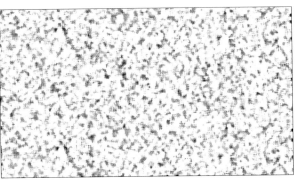

STEP 2. Bunching the Noise Particles

Choose Filter, Noise, Median from the menu bar to open the Median dialog box. Set the Radius to 4, and then click OK to bunch the noise particles.

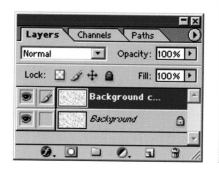
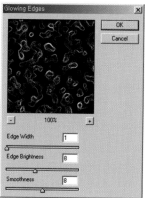

STEP 3. Making the Bacteria Outlines

Copy the Background layer by dragging it onto the Create a new layer button on the Layers palette. With the new Background copy layer selected in the Layers palete, choose Filter, Stylize, Glowing Edges from the menu bar to open the Glowing Edges dialog box. Choose the settings shown here, and then click OK to define the edges of the organisms.

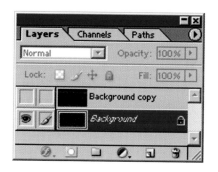

STEP 4. Detailing the Bacteria

Click the eye icon beside the Background copy layer in the Layers palette to hide the layer. Click the Background layer in the Layers palette to select that layer. Choose Image, Adjustments, Invert (Ctrl/Command+I) to invert the layer's colors.

STEP 5. Blurring the Background Layer

With the Background layer still selected in the Layers palette, choose Filter, Blur, Gaussian Blur from the menu bar to open the Gaussian Blur dialog box. Set the Radius to 3.2, and then click OK to blur the layer.

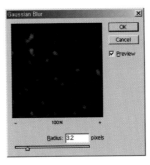

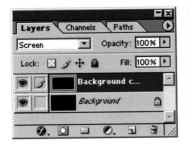

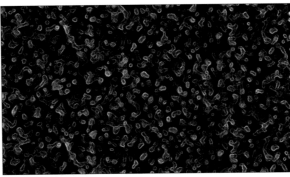

STEP 6. Blending the Bacteria Layer

Click the Background copy layer in the Layers palette to both redisplay and select the layer. Open the Layer Style drop-down list from the upper-left corner of the Layers palette, and then click Screen. The bacteria take on a more distinct appearance.

STEP 7. Adding Color to the Image

Click the Background layer in the Layers palette to select that layer, and then click the eye icon beside the Background copy layer to hide that layer from view. Choose Image, Adjustments, Hue/Saturation (Ctrl/Command+U) to open the Hue/Saturation dialog box. Click the Colorize check box to check it, drag the sliders to specify the settings shown here, and then click OK to add golden yellow tones to the layer.

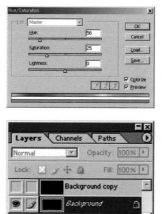

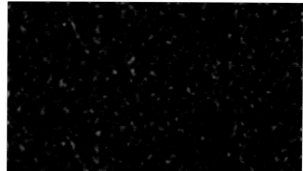

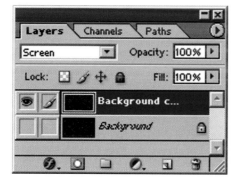

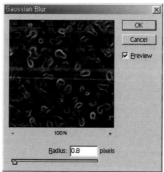

STEP 8. Softening the Outline of the Bacteria

Click the eye icon beside the Background layer on the Layers palette to hide that layer from view. Click the Background copy layer in the Layers palette to both redisplay and select the layer. Choose Filter, Blur, Gaussian Blur from the menu bar to open the Gaussian Blur dialog box. Set the Radius to 0.8, and then click OK to soften the contours of the image.

STEP 9. Adding Color to the Bacteria

With the Background copy layer still selected in the Layers palette, choose Image, Adjustments, Hue/Saturation (Ctrl/Command+U) to open the Hue/Saturation dialog box.

Click the Colorize check box to check it, drag the sliders to specify the settings shown here, and then click OK to add a blue tone to the layer.

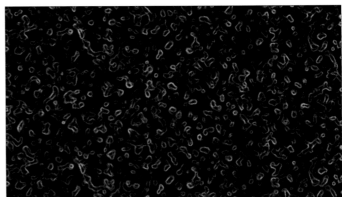

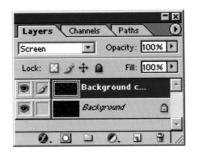

STEP 10. Redisplaying the Background

Click the eye icon box beside the Background layer in the Layers palette to redisplay the layer. The two layers blend together to make the bacteria look more realistic.

STEP 11.
Doubling the Image Size

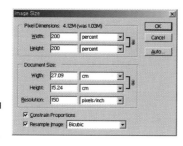

Choose Image,
Image Size
from the menu
bar to open
the Image Size
dialog box. In the Pixel Dimensions area of
the dialog box, choose Percent from the
Width drop-down list, and then enter 200 in
the Width text box. Also change the Height settings to 200 percent, and then
click OK to double the image size. Choose the Lasso tool from the toolbox, and
use it to select a few of the bacteria, as shown here.

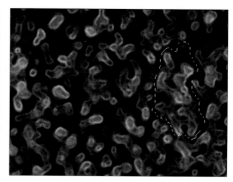

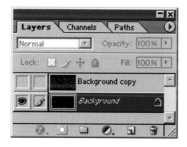

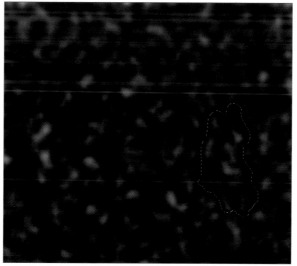

STEP 12. Adding Color to the Selected Bacteria

Click the eye icon beside the
Background copy layer in the Layers
palette to hide the layer from view,
and then click the Background layer
to select that layer. Choose Image,
Adjustments, Hue/Saturation
(Ctrl/Command+U) from the menu
bar to open the Hue/Saturation
dialog box. Choose the settings
shown here, and then click OK to
color the selected bacteria red.

STEP 13. Adding Color to the Outlines of the Selected Bacteria

Click the eye icon beside the Background layer in the Layers palette to hide the layer from view, and then click the Background copy layer to both redisplay and select that layer.

  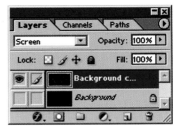

Choose Image, Adjustments, Hue/Saturation (Ctrl/Command+U) from the menu bar to open the Hue/Saturation dialog box. Choose the settings shown here, and then click OK to make the outlines of the bacteria a darker blue. Choose Select, Deselect (Ctrl/Command+D) from the menu bar to remove the selection marquee.

STEP 14. Merging the Layers

Click the eye icon box beside the Background layer in the Layers palette to redisplay the layer. Click the palette menu button in the upper-right corner of the Layers palette, and then click Merge Visible to merge both layers onto the Background layer. Copy the Background layer by dragging it onto the Create a new layer button on the Layers palette.

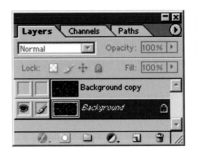 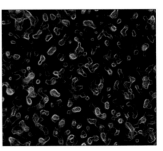

 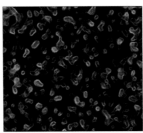

STEP 15. Sharpening the Background Layer

Click the eye icon beside the Background copy layer in the Layers palette to hide the layer from view, and then click the Background layer to select that layer. Choose Filter, Sharpen, Sharpen from the menu bar. Press Ctrl/Command+F three times to reapply the filter and further sharpen the image.

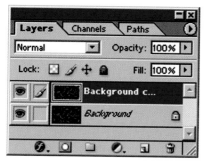

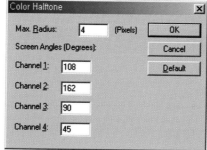

STEP 16. Coloring the Background Copy Layer

Click the Background copy layer in the Layers palette to both redisplay and select the layer. Choose Filter, Pixelate, Color Halftone from the menu bar to open the Color Halftone dialog box. Choose the settings shown here, and then click OK to display the layer content as colored dots.

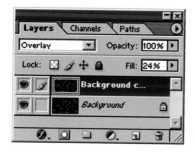

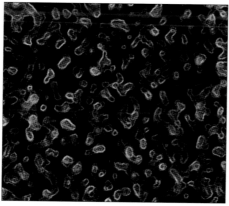

STEP 17. Blending the Layers

With the Background copy layer still selected in the Layers palette, open the Layer Style drop-down list from the upper-left corner of the Layers palette, and then click Overlay. Use the Fill slider on the Layers palette to change the Background copy layer's Fill value to 24%. The layers blend, making the image look like it's seen through an electron microscope.

STEP 18. Cropping the Image

Choose the Rectangular Marquee tool from the toolbox, drag on the image to select the portion to use in the final composition, and then choose Image, Crop from the menu bar to remove areas outside the selection from the image. Choose Select, Deselect (Ctrl/Command+D) from the menu bar to remove the selection marquee.

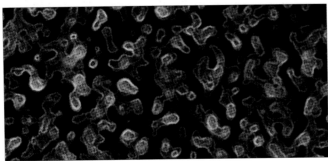

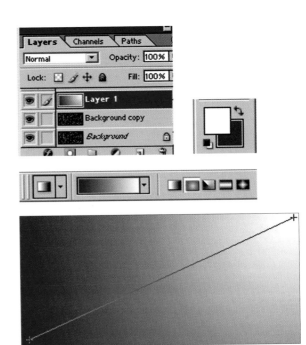

STEP 19. Adding a Gradient to a New Layer

Click the Create a new layer button (Shift+Ctrl/Command+N) on the Layers palette to add a new layer named Layer 1. After setting the foreground color to white and the background color to dark blue gray using the Color palette, choose the Gradient tool from the toolbox. Click the Radial Gradient button on the Options bar, and then drag from the upper-right corner of the image down to the lower-left corner as shown here to apply a radial gradient.

STEP 20. Blending the Gradient

With the Layer 1 layer still selected in the Layers palette, open the Layer Style drop-down list from the upper-left corner of the Layers palette, and then click Multiply. Use the Opacity slider on the Layers palette to change the Layer 1 layer's Fill value to 72%.

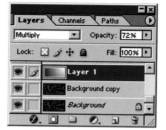

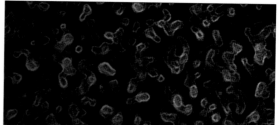

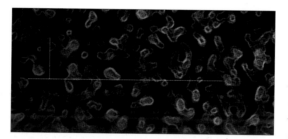

STEP 21. Completing the Image

Click the Create a new layer button on the Layers palette to add a new layer named Layer 2. Use the Color palette to set the foreground color to yellow. Choose the Pencil tool from the toolbox, and then use the Brush Preset picker from the Options bar to set the brush size to 1 px. To draw straight lines as shown here, press and hold the Shift key while dragging. Complete the image by using the Horizontal Type tool to add the text, using the lines as guides.

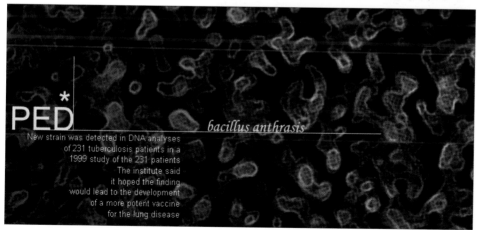

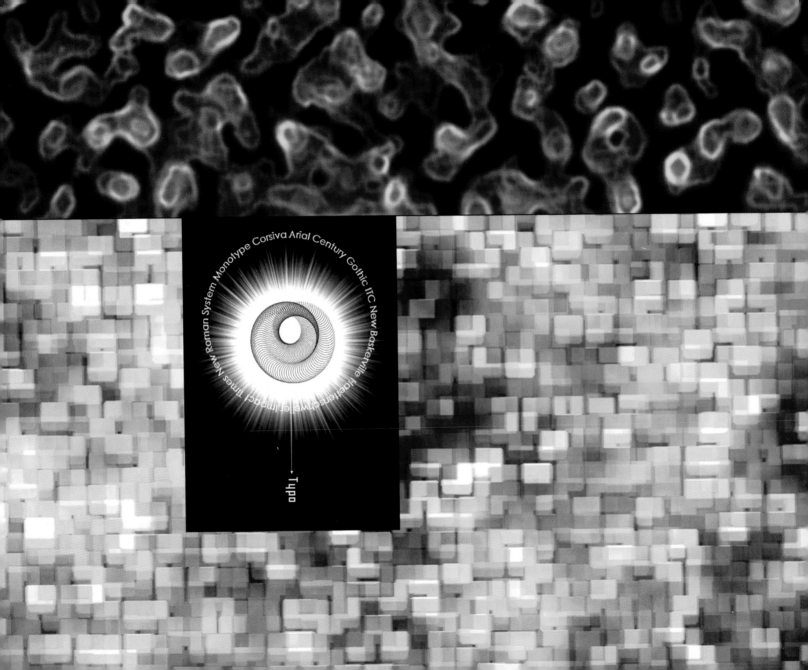

Project 24: Hard Light Effect

In this project, arrange objects made using a variety of techniques on a hard light image to create a spectacular graphic image. Adding a slight cyan tone will add an elegant tint to the finished image.

Hard Light Effect

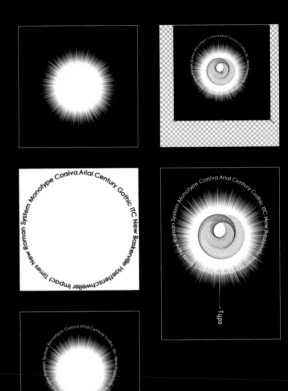

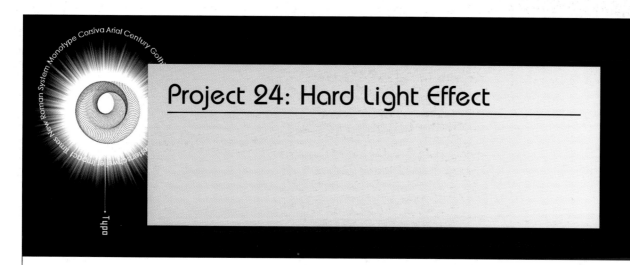

Project 24: Hard Light Effect

Total Steps

STEP 1. Making Half the New Image Black
STEP 2. Adding a Wind Blast
STEP 3. Adding More Wind
STEP 4. Rotating the Image 90°
STEP 5. Creating the Light Burst
STEP 6. Expanding the Light Burst
STEP 7. Entering Text
STEP 8. Arranging Text at the Bottom of the Image
STEP 9. Rolling the Text
STEP 10. Inverting the Text Color
STEP 11. Blending the Text Layer
STEP 12. Adding Blue Tones to the Light

STEP 13. Drawing a Circular Path
STEP 14. Duplicating the Circular Path
STEP 15. Completing the S-Shaped Path
STEP 16. Stroking the S-Shaped Path
STEP 17. Saving the Stroke as a Brush
STEP 18. Drawing a Circular Path
STEP 19. Adding Rotation to the Brush
STEP 20. Stroking the Circular Path with the S-Shaped Brush
STEP 21. Arranging the Image Layers
STEP 22. Decreasing the Image Size
STEP 23. Adding a Black Background Layer
STEP 24. Cropping the Image

STEP 1. Making Half the New Image Black

Choose File, New (Ctrl/Command+N) from the menu bar to open the New dialog box. Set the Width and Height to 800 pixels. Set the Resolution to 150 pixels/inch, make sure that White is selected under Contents, and click OK to create a new image. Click the Default Foreground and Background Colors button on the toolbox to set the foreground color to black and the background color to white.

Choose the Rectangular Marquee tool from the toolbox, and then drag to select the right half of the image as shown here. Use the Paint Bucket tool or press Alt/Option+Del to fill the selection with black. Choose Select, Deselect (Ctrl/Command+D) from the menu bar to remove the selection marquee.

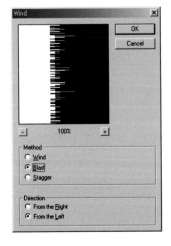
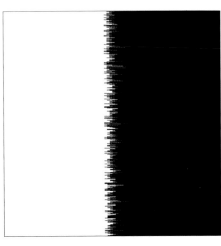

STEP 2. Adding a Wind Blast

Select Filter, Stylize, Wind from the menu bar to open the Wind dialog box. Click the Blast option button under Method, click From the Left under Direction, and then click OK to add a wind blast effect where the black and white areas abut.

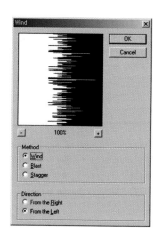

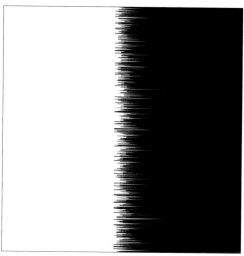

STEP 3. Adding More Wind

Choose Filter, Stylize, Wind again. Click the Wind option under Method, and then click OK to add detail to the wind blast effect. Press Ctrl/Command+F twice to apply the filter two more times.

STEP 4. Rotating the Image 90°

Double-click on the name of the Background layer in the Layers palette, and then click OK in the New Layer dialog box to convert the layer into a regular layer (named Layer 0) that you can edit at will. Choose Edit, Transform, Rotate 90° CW from the menu bar to rotate the image as shown here.

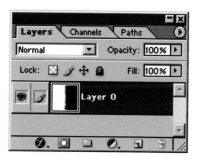

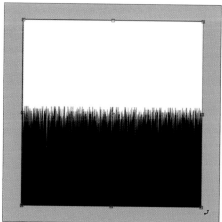

STEP 5. Creating the Light Burst

Choose Filter, Distort, Polar Coordinates from the menu bar to open the Polar Coordinates dialog box. Specify the settings shown here, and then click OK to create a circular light burst on the black background.

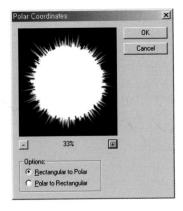

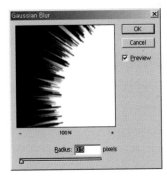

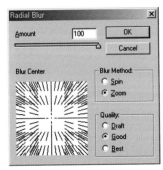

STEP 6. Expanding the Light Burst

Choose Filter, Blur, Gaussian Blur from the menu bar to open the Gaussian Blur dialog box. Choose the settings shown here, and then click OK to blur the light rays. Choose Filter, Blur, Radial Blur to open the Radial Blur dialog box. Specify the settings shown here, and then click OK to spread the light rays.

STEP 7. Entering Text

Click the Create a new layer button (Shift+Ctrl/Command+N) on the Layers palette to add a new layer. Click the Switch Foreground and Background Colors button on the toolbox to set the foreground color to white, and then use the Paint Bucket tool or press Alt/Option+Del to fill the new layer with white. Click the Default Foreground and Background Colors button on the toolbox to set the foreground color to black. Choose the Horizontal Type tool from the toolbox, click the Toggle the Character and Paragraph palettes button to open the Character palette if

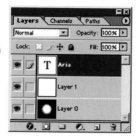

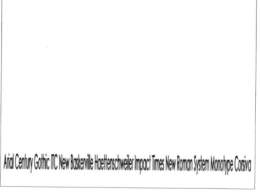

needed, and then use the Character palette to choose the settings shown here. Click in the image, type the text shown here at the bottom of the image, and then click the Commit any current edits button on the Options bar to finish adding the text. Choose Edit, Free Transform (Ctrl/Command+T), drag the handles that appear to size and position the text as shown here, and then press Enter/Return to finish the transformation.

STEP 8. Arranging Text at the Bottom of the Image

With the new text layer selected in the Layers palette, choose Edit, Transform, Rotate 180°. Click the palette menu button in the upper-right corner of the Layers palette, and then click Merge Down to merge the text onto the white Layer 1 layer.

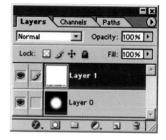

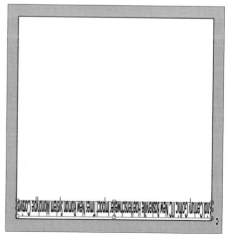

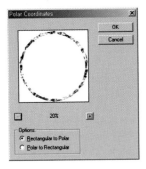

STEP 10. Inverting the Text Color

With the Layer 1 layer still selected in the Layers palette, choose Filter, Sharpen, Unsharp Mask from the menu bar to open the Unsharp Mask dialog box. Choose the settings shown here, and then click OK to bring the letters into focus. Choose Image, Adjustments, Invert (Ctrl/Command+I) to invert the layer color so it now has white text on a black background.

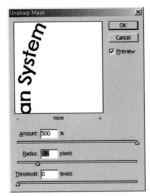

STEP 9. Rolling the Text

Choose Filter, Distort, Polar Coordinates from the menu bar to open the Polar Coordinates dialog box. Choose the settings shown here, and then click OK to roll the text into a circle.

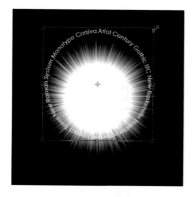
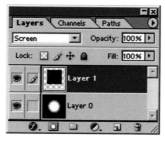

STEP 11. Blending the Text Layer

With Layer 1 still selected in the Layers palette, open the Layer Style drop-down list from the upper-left corner of the Layers palette, and then click Screen. If desired, choose Edit, Transform, Scale from the menu bar, drag the handles that appear to resize and reposition the text as shown here, and then press Enter/Return to finish the transformation.

STEP 12. Adding Blue Tones to the Light

Click the Layer 0 layer in the Layers palette to select that layer. Choose Image, Adjustments, Hue/Saturation (Ctrl/Command+U) from the menu bar to open the Hue/Saturation dialog box. Click the Colorize check box to check it, drag the sliders to specify the settings shown here, and then click OK to add a blue tint to the light burst.

STEP 13. Drawing a Circular Path

Click the Create a new layer button (Shift+Ctrl/Command+N) on the Layers palette to add a new layer named Layer 2. Drag the Layer 2 layer to the top of the Layers palette. Click the Switch Foreground and Background Colors button on the toolbox to set the foreground color. Use the Paint Bucket tool or press Alt/Option+Del to fill the new layer with white. Choose the Ellipse tool from the toolbox, click the Paths button in the Options bar, press and hold the Shift key, and then drag in the image window to draw a perfect circular path.

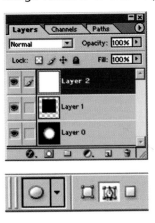
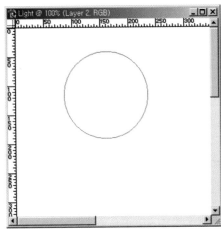

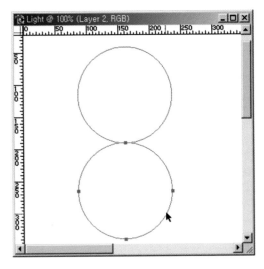

STEP 14. Duplicating the Circular Path

Choose the Path Selection tool from the toolbox, click the circular path in the image window, press and hold the Alt/Option key, and drag down in the image window to copy the circular path. Use the Path Selection tool to position the path copy as shown here.

STEP 15. Completing the S-Shaped Path

Choose the Direct Selection tool from the toolbox. Click each unneeded point on the path twice to select it, and then press Del to remove the point and the adjoining path segments. This converts the two circular paths into a single S-shaped path. Choose another toolbox tool when you finish editing the path to deselect the Direct Selection tool.

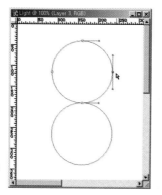 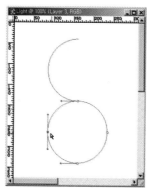 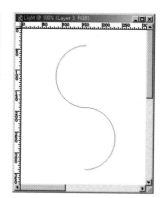

STEP 16. Stroking the S-Shaped Path

Click the Create a new layer button (Shift+Ctrl/Command+N) on the Layers palette to add a new layer named Layer 3. Choose Window, Paths to open the Paths palette, where you can see the S-shaped path you created: the Work Path. Click the Default Foreground and Background Colors button on the toolbox to set the foreground color to black. Choose the Pencil tool from the toolbox. Choose the Brush tool from the toolbox. Click the Click to open the Brush Preset picker button on the Options bar, drag the Master Diameter slider to set the brush size to 1 px, and then click the Click to open the Brush Preset picker button again to close the preset picker. Click the Stroke path with brush button on the Paths palette, which uses the selected brush to paint over the path shape. Click in a gray area on the Paths palette to deselect the path, and then choose Window, Layers to return to the Layers palette.

 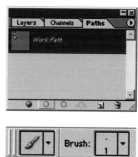 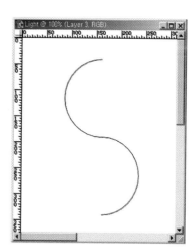

STEP 17. Saving the Stroke as a Brush

With the Layer 3 layer still selected in the Layers palette, choose Select, Load Selection from the menu bar. Make sure Layer 3 Transparency is selected from the Channel drop-down list, and then click OK to select the stroke on the layer. Choose Edit, Define Brush from the menu bar to open the Brush Name dialog box. Type "Light" as the name for the brush, and then click OK to save the shape as a brush. Choose Select, Select All (Ctrl/Command+A), press Del to remove the stroke from the layer, and then choose Select, Deselect (Ctrl/Command+D) from the menu bar to remove the selection marquee.

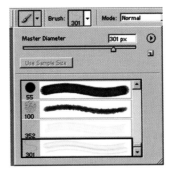

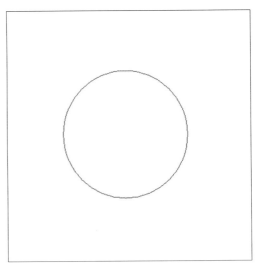

STEP 18. Drawing a Circular Path

Choose the Ellipse tool from the toolbox, click the Paths button in the Options bar, press and hold the Shift key, and then drag in the image window to draw a perfect circular path. Make the path about half the size of the image. Choose the Brush tool from the toolbox. The Brush you saved in Step 17 should be selected. Click the Click to open the Brush Preset picker button on the Options bar, drag the Master Diameter slider to set the brush size to 301 px, and then click the Click to open the Brush Preset picker button again to close the preset picker.

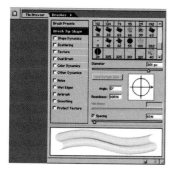
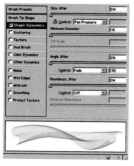

STEP 19. Adding Rotation to the Brush

Click the Toggle the Brushes palette button on the Options bar to open the Brushes palette. Click Brush Tip Shape in the list at the left, and set the Spacing to 10%. This makes a tight, S-shaped brush. Click Shape Dynamics in the list at the left. Choose Fade from the Control drop-down list under Angle Jitter, and then enter 170. These settings will cause the S-shaped brush to rotate slowly, making one rotation for every 170 repetitions of the S stroke. Click the palette close button to close the Brushes palette.

STEP 20. Stroking the Circular Path with the S-Shaped Brush

Delete the Layer 3 layer by dragging the layer onto the Delete layer button on the Layers palette. Click the Create a new layer button (Shift+Ctrl/Command+N) on the Layers palette to add a new layer named Layer 2. Choose Window, Paths to open the Paths palette. The circular path you drew earlier now appears as the Work Path. Click the Work Path to select it, if needed, and then click the Stroke path with brush button on the Paths palette. If a gap appears near the top, work with the brush rotation to correct it. Press Ctrl/Command+Z to undo the brush stroke, reopen the Brushes palette, and try another value in the Control text box. Click the Stroke path with brush button in the Paths palette to try the new repeat value. Click below the Work path in the Paths palette to hide the path, and then choose Window, Layers to return to the Layers palette.

STEP 21. Arranging the Image Layers

Delete Layer 2 by dragging the layer onto the Delete layer button in the Layers palette. Click the Layer 3 layer to select it in the Layers palette. Choose Edit, Free Transform (Ctrl/Command+T) from the menu bar. Drag the handles that appear to resize and rotate the stroked circle as shown here, and then press Enter/Return to finish the transformation.

STEP 22. Decreasing the Image Size

With the Layer 3 layer still selected in the Layers palette, click the box icon beside each of the two layers below to display a chain link, indicating that you've linked all the layers. Choose Edit, Transform, Scale from the menu bar, drag the handles that appear to reduce the size of the image and position it as shown here, and then press Enter/Return to finish the transformation.

STEP 23. Adding a Black Background Layer

Click the Create a new layer button (Shift+Ctrl/Command+N) on the Layers palette to add a new layer named Layer 4. Drag Layer 4 to the bottom of the Layers palette. With the foreground color set to black, use the Paint Bucket tool or press Alt/Option+Del to fill the new layer with black.

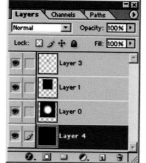

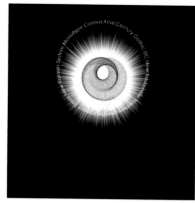

STEP 24. Cropping the Image

Choose the Rectangular Marquee tool from the toolbox. Drag to select the portion of the image you want to use in the final composition, and then choose Image, Crop from the menu bar to delete areas outside the selection. Choose Select, Deselect (Ctrl/Command+D) from the menu bar to remove the selection marquee. Add some simple text and ornamentation to complete the image.

difference

Most of us
naturally
resist
that
change

Project 25: Backlighted Shot

In this project, create an image with people illuminated by a back light. Only a black silhouette, with blurred edges due to the powerful effect of the light, portrays the people. Use the Gaussian Blur filter and Levels command to create this realistic and powerful image.

Backlighted Shot

Project 25: Backlighted Shot

difference

Most of us
naturally
resist
that
change

Total Steps

STEP 1. Opening the Source Photos
STEP 2. Selecting the Contours of the First Figure
STEP 3. Making the First Silhouette
STEP 4. Selecting the Contours of the Second Figure
STEP 5. Making the Second Silhouette
STEP 6. Copying the Silhouettes to a New Image
STEP 7. Adding Shadows to the Figures
STEP 8. Merging the Layers
STEP 9. Adding the Illuminated Door Layer
STEP 10. Diffusing the Light
STEP 11. Merging the Door Layers
STEP 12. Blending the Figures

STEP 13. Selecting the Light Shape
STEP 14. Redisplaying Layer 0
STEP 15. Blurring the Figures against the Light Shape
STEP 16. Blurring the Image
STEP 17. Thinning the Figures
STEP 18. Merging the Layers
STEP 19. Adding a Red Tone to the Image
STEP 20. Adding a New Layer with Cloud Texture
STEP 21. Adding Refraction to the Cloud Texture
STEP 22. Making the Cloud Texture Red
STEP 23. Blending the Cloud Texture
STEP 24. Adding Text to Complete the Image

photo_01.jpg

STEP 1. Opening the Source Photos

Choose File, Open (Ctrl/Command+O)
and open the Book\Sources\photo_01.jpg
and Book\Sources\photo_02.jpg files
from the supplementary CD-ROM.

STEP 2. Selecting the Contours of the First Figure

Go to the photo_01.jpg image, and then choose the Polygonal
Lasso tool from the toolbox. Select the shape of the person as
shown here. The selection does not need to be exact.

photo_02.jpg

STEP 3. Making the First Silhouette

Click the Create a new layer button
(Shift+Ctrl/Command+N) on the Layers palette to add a
new layer named Layer 1. Click the Default Foreground
and Background Colors button on the toolbox to set the
foreground color to black, and then use the Paint Bucket
tool or press Alt/Option+Del to fill the selection with black.

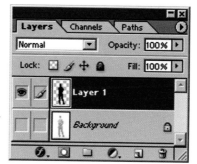

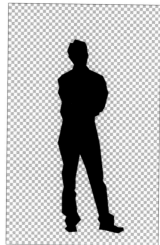

STEP 4. Selecting the Contours of the Second Figure

Go to the photo_02.jpg image, and then choose the Polygonal Lasso tool from the toolbox.
Select the shape of the person as shown here. Make the neck narrower to emphasize the
silhouette due to the backlight. Press and hold the Alt/Option key while specifying the
space between the arms and the torso to remove those areas from the selection.

STEP 5. Making the Second Silhouette

Click the Create a new layer button (Shift+Ctrl/Command+N) on the Layers palette to add a new layer named Layer 1. Click the Default Foreground and Background Colors button on the toolbox to set the foreground color to black, and then use the Paint Bucket tool or press Alt/Option+Del to fill the selection with black.

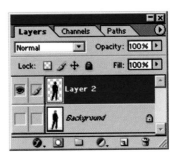

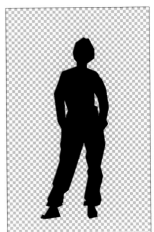

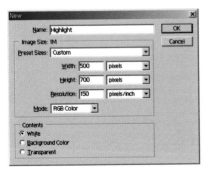

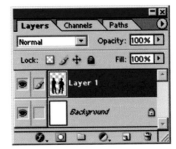

STEP 6. Copying the Silhouettes to a New Image

Choose File, New (Ctrl/Command+N) from the menu bar to open the New dialog box. Set the Width to 500 pixels and the Height to 700 pixels. Set the Resolution to 150 pixels/inch, make sure that White is selected under Contents, and click OK to create a new image. Choose the Move tool from the toolbox, and then copy each of the silhouettes you created by dragging from its layer (Layer 1) in the source image file onto the new image you just created. (You can then close the source image files.) Each silhouette appears on its own new layer in the Layers palette. Choose Edit, Free Transform (Ctrl/Command+T), use the handles that appear to adjust the size and position of the silhouettes, and then press Enter/Return. Press Ctrl/Command+E to merge the two silhouette layers onto a single layer named Layer 1.

  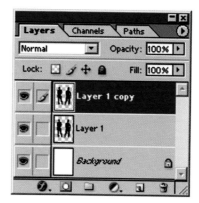

STEP 7. Adding Shadows to the Figures

Copy the Layer 1 layer by dragging it onto the Create a new layer button on the Layers palette. With the new Layer 1 copy layer selected, choose Edit, Transform, Perspective from the menu bar. Drag the top corner handles down to flip the silhouettes, and drag the handles to adjust the shadow shape as shown here. Drag the shadow into position, and then press Enter/Return to finish the transformation.

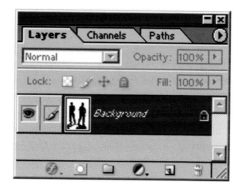

STEP 8. Merging the Layers

Click the palette menu button in the upper-right corner of the Layers palette, and then click Flatten Image to merge all the layers onto the Background layer.

STEP 9. Adding the Illuminated Door Layer

Click the Create a new layer button (Shift+Ctrl/Command+N) on the Layers palette to add a new layer named Layer 1. With the foreground color still set to black, use the Paint Bucket tool or press Alt/Option+Del to fill the new layer with black. Click the Create a new layer button again to add a new layer named Layer 2. Choose the Rectangular Marquee tool from the toolbox, and then draw a door shape in the upper-right corner of the image window. Click the Switch Foreground and Background Colors button on the toolbox to set the foreground color to white, and then use the Paint Bucket tool or press Alt/Option+Del to fill the selection with white on the Layer 2 layer. Choose Select, Deselect (Ctrl/Command+D) from the menu bar to remove the selection marquee.

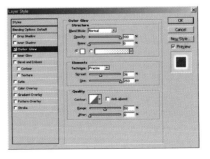

STEP 10. Diffusing the Light

With the Layer 2 layer still selected in the Layers palette, click the Add a layer style button at the bottom of the Layers palette, and then click Outer Glow. Choose the settings shown here in the Layer Style dialog box, and then click OK to add a glow to the layer.

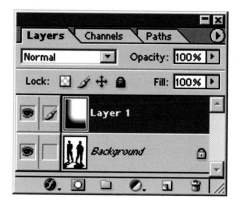

STEP 11. Merging the Door Layers

With the Layer 2 layer still selected in the Layers palette, click the palette menu button in the upper-right corner of the Layers palette. Click Merge Down in the menu that appears to merge the Layer 1 and Layer 2 layers into a single layer named Layer 1.

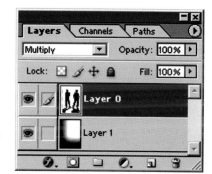

STEP 12. Blending the Figures

Double-click on the name of the Background layer in the Layers palette, and then click OK in the New Layer dialog box to convert the layer into a regular layer (named Layer 0) that you can edit at will. Drag Layer 0 to the top of the Layers palette. With Layer 0 still selected in the Layers palette, open the Layer Style drop-down list from the upper-left corner of the Layers palette, and then click Multiply to blend the two layers.

STEP 13. Selecting the Light Shape

Click the eye icon beside Layer 0 in the Layers palette to hide that layer. Choose Window, Channels to open the Channels palette. Ctrl/Command-click on the RGB channel to make a selection in the shape of the bright areas in the image. Choose Window, Layers to redisplay the Layers palette.

STEP 14. Redisplaying Layer 0

Click the eye icon box beside Layer 0 in the Layers palette to redisplay the layer. Also click the layer to select it, if needed.

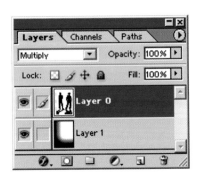

STEP 15. Blurring the Figures against the Light Shape

With Layer 0 still selected in the Layers palette, choose Filter, Blur, Gaussian Blur to open the Gaussian Blur dialog box. Set the Radius to 7.8, and then click OK to blur the edges of the silhouette. The Gaussian Blur filter is only applied to the bright areas of the image due to the selection frame. In other words, the outline of the silhouette is clear in the darker areas of the image, but blurred where it is surrounded by light.

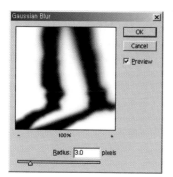

STEP 16. Blurring the Image

Choose Select, Deselect (Ctrl/Command+D) from the menu bar to remove the selection marquee. Choose Filter, Blur, Gaussian Blur from the menu bar to open the Gaussian Blur dialog box. Set the Radius to 3, and then click OK to blur all of Layer 0.

STEP 17. Thinning the Figures

With Layer 0 still selected in the
Layers palette, choose Image,
Adjustments, Levels (Ctrl/Command+L)
from the menu bar to open the Levels
dialog box. Drag the Input Levels
sliders to the positions shown here,
and then click OK to minimize the
black areas in the image, thinning
the silhouettes.

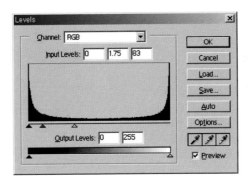

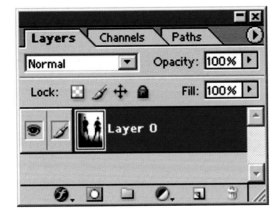

STEP 18. Merging the Layers

Click the palette menu button in the upper-right
corner of the Layers palette, and then click
Merge Down in the menu that appears to merge
the layers to a single layer named Layer 1.

STEP 19. Adding a Red Tone to the Image

Click the Default Foreground and Background Colors button on the toolbox to reset the colors. Choose Image, Adjustments, Gradient Map to open the Gradient Map dialog box. Click the gradient in the Gradient Used for Grayscale Mapping box of the Gradient Map dialog box to open the Gradient Editor dialog box. Click the first gradient preset in the Presets area, and then create four more color stops at the bottom of the gradient preview to include additional gradient colors. To set up a stop, click the bottom of the gradient preview, and then use the Color box at the bottom of the dialog box to choose the color for that stop. Drag the far right color stop left to move it to the position shown here. (You can delete a color stop by dragging it down off the bottom of the preview.) Click OK to close the Gradient Editor dialog box, and then click OK again to apply the gradient.

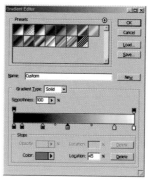

STEP 20. Adding a New Layer with Cloud Texture

Click the Create a new layer button (Shift+Ctrl/Command+N) on the Layers palette to add a new layer named Layer 2. Choose Filter, Render, Clouds from the menu bar to add a black and white cloud texture on the new layer. Choose Filter, Render, Difference Clouds to blend another cloud texture on the layer. Press Ctrl/Command+F two or three times to reapply the Difference Clouds filter, creating a more complex cloud texture.

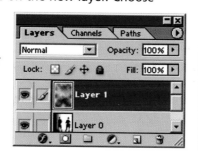
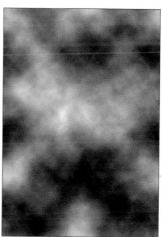

STEP 21. Adding Refraction to the Cloud Texture

With the Layer 2 layer still selected in the Layers palette, choose Filter, Distort, Ocean Ripple from the menu bar to open the Ocean Ripple dialog box. Choose the settings shown here, and then click OK to apply the filter.

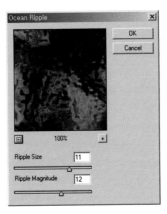

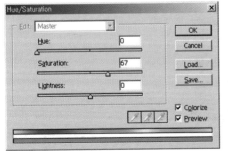

STEP 22. Making the Cloud Texture Red

With the Layer 2 layer still selected in the Layers palette, choose Image, Adjustments, Hue/Saturation (Ctrl/Command+U) from the menu bar to open the Hue/Saturation dialog box. Click the Colorize check box to check it, drag the Saturation slider to the setting shown here, and then click OK to change the color of the cloud texture to red.

STEP 23. Blending the Cloud Texture

With the Layer 2 layer still selected in the Layers palette, open the Layer Style drop-down list from the upper-left corner of the Layers palette, and then click Overlay. Use the Fill slider on the Layers palette to change the Fill value for Layer 2 to 80%.

STEP 24. Adding Text to Complete the Image

Choose the Rectangular Marquee tool from the toolbox, select the area of the image to use in the final composition, and then choose Image, Crop from the menu bar to remove areas outside the selection. Use the Horizontal Type tool and Character palette to add text in a simple font to complete the image.